T
Welsh
REVIVAL

Part 1

A Narrative Of Facts

By
William T. Stead,
Editor of Review of Reviews, London
And

Part 2

The Revival: Its Power and Source

By Rev. G. Campbell Morgan,
Pastor: Westminster Chapel, London

****

The Story of The

Welsh Revival

**As Told by Eyewitnesses Together With a Sketch of
Evan Roberts and His Message to The World**

By
Arthur Goodrich, Evan Roberts, Rev. G. Campbell Morgan, W.
T. Stead, Rev. Evan Hopkins, and others

Trumpet Press, Lawton, OK

Both books first published in 1905.

Edition 1.0, July 2015

Copyright © 2015 by Trumpet Press, Lawton, OK all rights reserved

Authors: Stead, William T. and Morgan, G. Campbell; Goodrich, Arthur and Roberts, Evans.

Title: The Welsh Revival & The Story of the Welsh Revival
  1. Christian History 2. Revival 3. Rituals and Practice

  ISBN-13: 978-0692498057
  ISBN-10: 0692498052

Trumpet Press is a member of the Christian Small Publishers Association (CSPA).

Table of Contents

The Welsh Revival

Part 1,

A Narrative Of Facts

By William T. Stead,

Part 2:

By Rev. G. Campbell Morgan

****

Book Two:

The Story of The Welsh Revival

About the Authors

William T. Stead was an English newspaper editor who was greatly influenced by his personal experience at the revival, and used his paper, *The Pall Mall Gazette,* to promote the revival. He was a pioneer of investigative journalism, and died with the sinking of the Titanic.

Rev. G. Campbell Morgan was pastor of Westminster Chapel in London, and author of several books and Bible commentaries.

Evan Roberts was the founder of the 1904-1905 revival in Wales that transformed the nation. He was forced to stop the meeting because of exhaustion. Then became editor of a Christian magazine.

A Note From the Publisher

These books were both first published in 1905. Some of the words have been updated to modern spelling, but some words have not, and there are also some Welsh words that are very oddly spelled.

The first book starts out sounding like it might be about the first revival in Wales in 1859-60, but he is just starting with that as back -ground information.

Also from Trumpet Press

The Kentucky Revival, by Richard McNemar

The Coming Prince, by Sir Robert Anderson

Discoveries in Bible Prophecy, by Michael D. Fortner

The Beast and False Prophet Revealed, by Michael D. Fortner

The Fall of Babylon the Great America, by Michael D. Fortner

Chapter 1
From The Author To The Reader

This is the reason why this little book is written:

I am a child of the Revival of 1859 - 60. I have witnessed the Revival in South Wales, and it is borne in upon me that I must testify as to what I have seen and know.

I have been urged and entreated to speak in public on the subject. I have refused, although sorely tempted to comply. But though I am not physically strong enough to face the immense strain which public speaking always makes upon my nervous system, I cannot keep silent. Woe is me if I bear not my testimony, and bear it now! For never is it so true as in times of Revival that Now is the accepted time. "Now is the day of salvation."

That is not a mere hackneyed text; it is a somewhat awe-inspiring fact. A fact, not a theory. The importance of the psychological moment so much insisted upon by Bismarck is as true in religion as in politics. It is the familiar truth, which all admit in other departments of life.

> "There is a tide in the affairs of men
> Which, taken at the flood, leads on to fortune.
> Omitted, all the voyage of their life
> Is bound in shallows, and in miseries."

Let me preface my narrative, as is the custom in all meetings when the awakened soul cries for facts from the experience of living men rather than for things at second-hand, by stating briefly how I came to be able to speak with knowledge of the mysterious force operating upon the heart of men which is in action at times of Revival.

I first woke up to a sense of my own sinfulness when I was a child of eleven. I was a child of the Manse. My father was an Independent minister, and both my parents were earnest, devoted Evangelical Christians. Independents sixty years ago were more Calvinistic than are their present-day representatives, and a sense of the exceeding sinfulness of sin and of the grim reality of the wrath of God permeated the atmosphere of our home. The higher the ideal of life and conduct to which we were taught to aspire, the more bitterly and constantly we were compelled to realize by every childish fault of selfishness or of temper how true it was that we had all sinned and come short of the glory of God. We were condemned by our own consciences. Even when we would do good, evil was present with us. How could we, with all our imperfections, our sins, and our short-comings, think without a shudder of the day when all secrets were revealed, and the soul, stripped bare of all wrappings and pretense, had to render account to its Maker for all the deeds that had been done in the body? It is the fashion of our day to regard such striving after the ideal as morbid; but although the phraseology may need revision, the essential truth remains the same.

It is not surprising, then, that one night, at eleven years of age, when I went to bed, I was seized with an appalling sense of my own unworthiness, my own exceeding sinfulness. God was so good, and I was so bad - I deserved to be damned. I accepted as a postulate the infinite goodness of God, and I knew only too well how often I had done the things I ought not to have done, and left undone the things I ought to have done, and that there was no strength in me. I sobbed and cried in the darkness with a vague sense of my own sin and of the terrible doom which awaited me. I had a passionate longing to escape from condemnation and be forgiven. At last my mother overheard me, took me into her arms, and told me comforting things about the love of God, and how it was made manifest by Jesus Christ, who had suffered in our stead, to save us from condemnation, and make us heirs of heaven. I have no remembrance of anything beyond the soothing caress of my mother's words. When she left me the terror had gone; and although I had not in any way experienced the change which is called conversion, I felt sufficiently tranquil to go to sleep. When I woke the memory of the previous night's alarm was but as the remembrance of a thunderstorm when it has passed.

This was in the year 1860, when the Revival which had begun in the United States of America in 1857 or 1858 crossed the Atlantic, traversed the north of Ireland in 1858, covered Wales in 1859, and then moved into England, where its influence was felt all through 1860 and 1861.

In July, 1861, I was sent to a boarding school for Congregational ministers" sons, to which some sons of laymen were also admitted, at Silcoates Hall, near Wakefield. There were about fifty of us boys, from ten years old to sixteen or seventeen. The tradition of the school in the fifties and in 1860 had not been distinctly religious. All of us came from Christian homes, but as a school it was very much like other schools. About a month after I entered Silcoates some of the lads started a prayer meeting of their own in a summerhouse in the garden. They asked me to join, and I went more out of curiosity, and to oblige my chum, than for any other motive. There were about half-a-dozen of us, perhaps more, none of us over fourteen. We read a chapter in the Bible, and we prayed. No master was present, nor was there any attempt made on the part of the masters to encourage the prayer meeting. One master, indeed, was frankly contemptuous. The majority of the boys had nothing to do with the prayer-meeting fellows. One or two of us were under deep conviction of sin, and we talked among ourselves, and read the Bible, and prayed. Suddenly one day, after the prayer meeting had been going on for a week or two, there seemed to be a sudden change in the atmosphere. How it came about no one ever knew. All that we did know was that there seemed to have descended from the sky, with the suddenness of a drenching thunder shower, a spirit of intense earnest seeking after God for the forgiveness of sins and consecration to His service. The summerhouse was crowded with boys. A deputation waited upon the principal, and told him what was happening. He was very sympathetic and helpful. Preparation class was dispensed with that night; all the evening the prayer meeting was kept going, There was no singing, only Bible reading, a few brief words of exhortation, a confession of sin, and asking for prayers, and ever and anon a joyful acknowledgement of an assurance of forgiveness. Those of us who could not find peace were taken out into the playground by one or two of their happier comrades, who labored with them to accept Christ. How well to this very day do I remember the solemn hush of that memorable day and night, in the course of which forty out of the fifty lads publicly professed conversion. Only half-a-dozen out of the whole school, and these exclusively of the oldest boys, held aloof from the movement, and were prayed for jointly and severally by name by their converted comrades.

I remember the way in which it came to me that my sins were forgiven, and that from being a rebel against God I was admitted into the family of the redeemed. I had no ecstasy. Alas! my temperament is not subject to ecstasies. My friend, a lad of my own age, was walking by my side plying me diligently with texts, and appealing to me to believe only in Christ. As we walked and talked together it slowly seemed to dawn upon my mind that I had been saved all the time, and had never known it till just then. Saved not by any merit of my own, but because in some mysterious way, positively asserted in the New Testament, and verified by the experience of all the best human beings whom I knew or had heard of, the death of Christ had reconciled the world to God. He had borne my sins, therefore they were no longer on record against me. There was no condemnation for those who were in Christ Jesus. And who were "in Christ Jesus"? The whole human race, excepting those who thrust themselves out of His fold, and would none of Him. In short, it seemed to me that I had always inverted the position. Instead of thinking I had to do some strange spiritual act described as coming to Jesus, when my sins would be forgiven and I should be adopted as a Son of God, I came to see that Christ had already reconciled me to God, had forgiven my sins, thousands of years before they had been committed, and that I had just to accept the position in which He had graciously placed me. Of my own self I could have done nothing. I was a sinner, not only in the sight of God, but in my own inner consciousness. I had been made in the image of God, and had unmade myself into the image of a very ordinary, bad -tempered, selfish lad, not perhaps more bad-tempered or more selfish than other twelve-year old lads, but a very ordinary sinner, not by any means the saint and the hero which I ought to have been. I was a poor wretch, but God in His unspeakable love and mercy had blotted out my sins, and taken me into junior - very junior - partnership with Himself. The terms were, on my side, that I had to do what He told, me, and, on His side, that He would tell me quite clearly what He wanted me to do. And although I had no ecstasy, and was gladdened by no heavenly vision, a sense of great peace and deliverance settled upon me.

I was seized with the longing to tell others of the discovery I had made - that we were saved all the time if we only knew it, and that God was a great deal more anxious to take us into partnership than we were to accept so gracious an offer. Writing was a sore cross to me, at 12, but I wrote to my parents and told them the good news. I wrote to my elder sister, urging her to be converted. We had prayer circles for the conversion of our unconverted comrades. In the fervor of my boyish zeal I decided to be a missionary, and applied myself all the more diligently to my lessons. About twenty of us joined the Church as communicants. Every night during the two years I was at Silcoates the prayer meeting was kept up by the lads. Half an hour after tea, before preparation, was given to the prayer meeting. But - and this brings me to the point of all this confession of personal experience - although the tone of the school was kept up at a high level, and although the prayer meeting was kept going, and the solid fruits of the Revival lasted all the time I was there, we never had another conversion after that strange outpouring of the Spirit which overwhelmed us all, unexpected, at the beginning of the term. Those who were brought in during the Revival week stood for the most part firm, those who stood out against the Revival never came in afterwards. Neither, so far as I remember, with perhaps one or two exceptions, did the new lads who entered school later on seek or find conversion.

I am not setting forth the conception of the relation between man and his Maker embodied in the foregoing narrative as if it were the truth of God to any other soul excepting my own. And for those who deny both God and the soul, I am willing, for the sake of argument, to admit that the whole episode in my life was nothing more or less than the delusion of something that imagined itself to be a soul as to the reality of its relations with a nullity which it imagined was its Creator. The truth or the falsehood of my notions is, in this immediate connection, quite immaterial. For what I am wanting to insist upon is, first, that these seasons of spiritual exaltation which we call Revivals are realities to those who come under their influence, permanently affecting their whole future lives; and, secondly, that they come like the wind and vanish as mysteriously, and that those who resist them may never again feel so potent a call to a higher life.

It is this sense of the fact that the Revival, when it comes, does not stop but passes on, which fills me with such a sense of the infinite importance of this present time, that I feel I must do what I can to bring to the knowledge of as many persons as I can reach, the glad tidings of great joy that a Revival of Religion is once more in our midst.

The old story of the man who was gathering eggs from the face of a precipitous cliff always recurs to me at such seasons of opportunity. The man, clinging to a rope, had lowered himself from the overhanging edge of a beetling cliff, till he was opposite the ledge where the seabirds laid their eggs. Owing to the extent to which the brow of the cliff overhung the sea, whose waves were dashing 203 feet below, the egg-gatherer found himself some ten feet distant from the ledge of the nests. By swaying to and fro, he was able to make himself swing as a pendulum outward and inward, until at last the extreme inward swing of the rope brought him to the ledge, on to which he sprang. As he did so he lost hold of the rope. There he stood for one awful moment midway between sea and sky. The rope swinging outward after he had quitted his hold was returning like a pendulum. It came, but not so far as to enable him to clutch it from where he stood. Outward it swung again, and he realized with agony that as each time it swayed to and fro it would be further and further off, until at last it would hang stationary far out of his reach. When the rope began slowly to swing inwards, he saw that the next time it would be out of his reach. Breathless, he waited until the rope was just about to pause before swinging back, then, knowing that it was now or never, he leapt into space, caught the rope, and was saved. Another second and he would have lost his chance. It is just so, it seems to me, with Revivals. They come and they go, and if they are not utilized the opportunity goes by - in some cases forever.

For the Churches the Revival is like spring. The good seed sown then springs up and bears fruit, whereas ten times the quantity of seed sown in winter's frost or summers heat would simply perish. But in these prefatory observations I am not thinking of the Churches so much as of the individual reader who does not believe, who is not converted, and who is only idly curious as to whether there is anything in this Revival business, or whether there is not. It is for them that I have told, for the first time in my life, the story of how a Revival affected me, and what I know of it at first hand. And there is one other point upon which I think I may fairly claim to speak at first hand, and that is as to the effect of that experience at Silcoates in 1861 upon my own life. Whatever may be the objective reality of the altered relations which I then recognized as existing between my soul and its Maker, there is absolutely no question as to the abiding nature of the change it effected in my life. It is forty-three years since that Revival at school. The whole of my life during all these forty-three years has been influenced by the change which men call conversion which occurred with me when I was twelve. My views as to many things have naturally broadened much in these forty-three years. But that was the conscious starting point of everything that there has been in my life of good or of service for my fellow-creatures. It was my first conversion. Other spiritual experiences, involving a wider conception of the reality of God in man, a deeper sense of the need for self-surrender, I have had, and hope yet to have. But the fundamental change, the conscious recognition of the fact that I had been most graciously allotted a junior partnership with God Almighty in the great task of making this world a little bit more like heaven than it is today, came to me then. My life has been flawed with many failures, darkened with many sins, but the thing in it which was good, which has enabled me to resist temptations to which I would otherwise have succumbed, to bear burdens which would otherwise have crushed me with their weight, and which has kept the soul within me ever joyfully conscious that, despite all appearances to the contrary, this is God's world, and that He and I are fellow-workers in the work of its renovation - that potent thing, whatever you may call it, and however you may explain it, came into my life there, and abides with me to this hour; - my one incentive and inspiration in this life; my sole hope for that which is to come.

Therefore I hope my reader will understand how it is that I, being a child of the Revival of 1858 to 1861, should hail with exceeding great joy the reappearance of the Revival in 1904. For as the mysterious out-powering of the blessing forty-three years ago has been of permanent help and strength and comfort to my own life ever since that time, so will this Revival in the West change, transform, inspire, and glorify the lives of multitudes who at present know nothing and care nothing for the things that make for their own peace and the welfare of their fellowmen.

And the thought that haunts me and will not let me rest until I send out this little book is that if I do not write it, and write it now, yon, my reader, may not hear the bugle call which is sounding in the West; the Revival may pass by, and, too late, you may awake to discover that you have missed the gift of God which it bore for your soul.

Chapter 2
The National Significance Of Revivals

Slowly the Bible of the race is writ,
And not on paper leaves nor leaves of stone,
Each age, each kindred adds a verse to it,
Texts of despair or hope, of joy or moan;
While swings the sea, while mists the mountains shroud,
While thunders surges burst on cliffs of cloud,
Still at the prophets feet the nations sit. - Lowell.

ONE of these newly written verses is spelling itself out before our very eyes in Wales. In order to understand its significance we need to look backward across some centuries to realize what vast issues may be in this upheaval among the Welsh country folk.

The word Revival is not to be found in the index to the latest edition of the "Encyclopedia Britannica". Neither does it figure in the comprehensive index to Baring-Goulds "Lives of the Saints". Yet the Saints were great Revivalists, and the history of the progress of the world is largely made up of the record of successive Revivals. The Revival of Religion has been the invariable precursor of social and political reform. This was very admirably put by the Rev. F. B. Meyer in his Presidential Address to the Ninth National Council of the Evangelical Free Churches at Newcastle-on-Tyne in 1904.

Every great Revival of religion has issued in social and political reconstruction. In no history has the effect of the one upon the other been more carefully traced than in Green's

"History of the English People." Take, for instance, his account of the Revival of the twelfth century. "At the close of Henry's reign," he says, "and throughout that of Stephen, England was stirred by the first of those great religious movements which it was afterwards to experience in the preaching of the Friars, the Lollardism of Wycliffe, the Reformation, the Puritan enthusiasm, and the mission work of the Wesleys. Everywhere, in town and country, men banded themselves together for prayer; hermits flocked to the woods; noble and churl welcomed the austere Cistercians as they spread over the moors and forests of the North. A new spirit of devotion woke the slumbers of the religious houses, and penetrated alike to the homes of the noble and the trader. The power of this Revival eventually became strong enough to wrest England from the chaos of feudal misrule after a long period of feudal anarchy, and laid the foundations of the Great Charta." We may go further, and assert that the movements which led to the abolition of the Slave Trade and the Com Laws originated in the evangelistic efforts of Wesley and Whitefield. Even Mr. Benjamin Kidd, in his "Social Evolution," lays great stress on the religious foundations upon which civilization rests. He tells us that the intellect has always mistaken the nature of religious forces, and regarded them as beneath its notice, though they had within them power to control the course of human development for hundreds and even thousands of years. Discussing the opposition of the educated classes in England to progress, he says: "The motive force behind the long list of progressive measures has not, to any appreciable extent, come from the educated classes - it has come almost exclusively from the middle and lower classes, who have in turn acted, not under the stimulus of intellectual motives, but under the influence of their religious feelings. It is, therefore, on the authority of history and economics that we base our contention that society can only be saved through a great Revival of Religion.

There are certain phenomena which precede and which follow Revivals of Religion. The symptoms premonitory of a Revival are the phenomena of death, corruption, and decay. It is ever the darkest hour before the dawn. The nation always seems to be given over to the Evil One before the coming of the Son of Man. The decay of religious faith, the deadness of the Churches, the atheism of the well-to-do, the brutality of the masses, all these, when at their worst, herald the approach of the Revival. Things seem to get too bad to last. The reign of evil becomes intolerable. Then the soul of the nation awakes.

That the familiar phenomena of the reign of sin are with us and abound, no serious observer will dispute. As a nation we have once more stooped to those depths of bloody mire in which from time to time Britain has wallowed. Drunkenness, gambling, and gluttony, with others of the seven deadly sins, abound. Worldliness is universal. High ideals are eclipsed. Plain living and high thinking are at a discount. To see as in a mirror the vacuous mind of a generation which eschews serious thought you have only to read the popular newspapers and periodicals of the day.

Life has become for the comfortable classes little better than a musical comedy. You look in vain for the strenuous, high-spirited youth who scorn delights and live laborious days in order to achieve something of good for their fellowmen. To have a good time is the end-all and be-all of millions. Indolence, indifference, and selfishness so dominate that even the healthy game of football has become little better than a modem substitute for the gladiatorial sports of ancient Rome -- the winter gambling bell that replaces the summer racecourse. Our young men do not play themselves, they look on while professionals play.

In politics degradation shows itself chiefly in the indifference to blood-shed and the waste of the resources of our own people in making believe to be ready to slaughter our neighbors. As a condemnation alike of the morality and intellect of the nation, the Army and Navy expenditure of Britain for the last twelve years stands without a parallel. Here we have the very note of the decadence of our time. That way madness lies, and the supreme and crowning demonstration of the criminal lunacy which has overtaken us is afforded by the proposal to tax the bread and sugar of the poor in order to meet the demands of insatiate Mars.

If, therefore, a Revival never comes until the nation has sunk into the slough of luxury and vice, and wallows in brutality and crime, then this precursory symptom is assuredly not wanting in the present situation. It is interesting to turn over the pages of Green's History of the English People and to note how invariably the Revival is preceded by a period of corruption and followed by a great advance in the direction of national progress.

Take, for instance, what he tells us about the state of England on the eve of the second Revival. The effect of the first Revival had passed away by the middle of the thirteenth century. The second was brought about by the Franciscans and the Dominicans.

Speaking of the coming of the Friars, Mr. Green says:

> The religious hold of the priesthood on the people was loosening day by day . . . . The disuse of preaching, the decline of the monastic orders into rich landowners, the non-residence and ignorance of the parish priests, robbed the clergy of their spiritual influence. The abuses of the times foiled even the energy of such men as Bishop Grosseteste, of Lincoln. To bring the world back again within the pale of the Church was the aim of two religious orders which sprang suddenly into life in the opening of the thirteenth century.

He then describes how the Revival due to the Black Friars of St. Dominic and the Grey Friars of St. Francis swept in a great tide of popular enthusiasm over the land. They carried the Gospel to the poor by the entire reversal of the Older Monasticism by seeking personal salvation in effort for the salvation of their fellowmen. Their fervid appeal, coarse wit, and familiar story brought religion into the fair and the market place. They captured the University of Oxford, and made it stand in the front line in its resistance to Papal ex-actions and its claim of English liberty:

> The classes in the towns on whom the influence of the Friars told most directly were the steady supporters of freedom throughout the Barons War. Adam Marsh was the closest

friend and confidant both of Grosseteste and Earl Simon of Montfort.

Thus, if the first Revival preceded the signing of the Magna Charta, the second paved the way for the assembly of the first English Parliament.

The third Revival mentioned by Green was that of Wycliffe. The second Revival had spent its force in a hundred years. The Church of the Middle Ages had, at the middle of the fourteenth century, sunk to its lowest point of spiritual decay. The clergy were worldly and corrupt, and paralyzed by their own dissensions. The early enthusiasm of the Friars had died away, leaving a crowd of impudent mendicants behind. Then Wycliffe arose. He recalled the ideal of the Kingdom of God before the eyes of mankind, and established his order of Simple Priests or Poor Preachers, who, with coarse speech and russet dress, preached the Gospel throughout the land with such success that the enemy declared in alarm that "every second man one meets is a Lollard". Wycliffe died, but the seed he had sowed sprang up and bore terrible fruit in the Peasant Revolt, which, although ultimately trampled out in bloodshed, was the first great warning given to the landlords of England that the serf not only had the rights of man, but was capable on occasion of asserting them, even by such extreme measures as the decapitation of an Archbishop.

The fourth Revival was that which preceded the Reformation. Tyndale, with his translation of the Bible, blew upon the smoldering embers of Lollardry and they burst into flame. The new Scriptures were disputed, rimed, sung, and jangled in every tavern and ale-house. From that revival of popular religion among the masses came by tortuous roads the triumph of Protestantism.

After the Reformation and the Renaissance had achieved their culminating glory in the reign of Queen Elizabeth, a period of decadence and of corruption set in under the Stuarts. Under James I, Whitehall became an Augean stable of all uncleanness, and a vicious Court assailed the liberties of England. Against this corruption in high places a fierce religious rebellion broke out amongst the serious English folk. The Puritan Revival of the first half of the seventeenth century had two notable offshoots. The first was the founding of New England by the men of the Mayflower; the other was the founding of the English Commonwealth by the Ironsides of Cromwell. The great struggle of the seventeenth century was primarily religious, only secondarily political. As Green remarks, "There was one thing dearer in England than free speech in Parliament, than security for property, or even personal liberty, and that one thing was, in the phrase of the day, the Gospel." It was the religious Revival that summoned Milton from literature to politics. So long as the question between King and Parliament was purely political, he shut himself up with his books and "calmly awaited the issue of the contest, which I trusted to the wise conduct of Providence and to the courage of the people." But when men began to demand the reforming of the Church in accordance with the Word of God, Milton tells us in his Second Defense of the People of England:

> This awakened all my attention and my zeal. I saw that a way was opening for the establishment of real liberty, that the foundation was laying for the deliverance of man from the yoke of slavery and superstition, that the principles of religion, which were the first objects of our care, would exert a salutary influence on the manners and constitution of the republic: and as I had from my youth studied the distinction between religious and civil rights, I perceived that if I ever wished to be of use I ought at least not to be wanting to my country, to the Church, and to so many of my fellow-Christians in a crisis of so much danger. I therefore determined to relinquish the other pursuits in which I was engaged, and to transfer the whole force of my talents and industry to this one important subject.

Others besides Milton felt the imperious call of the religious movement of his time. Nor did its impulse fail until the death of Oliver Cromwell opened the door to the rabble rout of the Restoration.

Once more England plunged heavily towards the nethermost

abyss, and once again a great Revival of Religion took place to save the soul of the nation from perdition. It was partly due to the relentless persecution of the Nonconformists, but it owed much also to the flaming zeal of the Quakers, who were the great Revivalists of the second half of the seventeenth century. The Government had at one time in horrible dungeons as many as four thousand of these excellent men. Professor William James truly says of the Quaker religion that it "is something which it is impossible to overpraise."

> In a day of shams, it was a religion of veracity rooted in spiritual inwardness and a return to something more like the original Gospel truth than men had ever known in England. So far as our Christian sects today are evolving into liberality, they are simply reverting in essence to the position which Fox and the early Quakers so long ago assumed.

The Quaker Revival had as its immediate political result the founding of Pennsylvania, and among its more remote and indirect effects the final expulsion of the Stuarts.

Quakerism, tolerated, lost much of the savory salt that it possessed when it was kept up to the standard of the apostles by the sufferings of the martyrs. The reversion of the English people, especially of the highest and the lowest, to sheer paganism is one of the most constant phenomena of our history. After the Stuarts had vanished and the Protestant succession secured, the land relapsed into brutality and infidelity in the eighteenth century, as it had done in every century since the Conquest.

Then came the seventh and best known Revival of all under Wesley and Whitefield. Once again England had gone rotten at the head. In the higher circles of society every one laughs, said Montesquieu on his visit to England, if one talks of religion. Of the prominent statesmen of the time, the greater part were unbelievers in any form of Christianity, and distinguished for the grossness and immorality of their lives. As at the top, so at the bottom. The masses were brutalized beyond belief. In London, at one time, gin-shops invited every passer-by to get drunk for a penny, and dead drunk for two-pence. But in the midst of this moral wilderness a religious Revival sprang up which carried to the hearts of the people a fresh spirit of moral zeal, while it purified our literature and our manners. "A new philanthropy reformed our prisons, infused clemency and wisdom into our penal laws, abolished the slave trade, and gave the first impulse to popular education." The Revival then was not without many features which caused the sinner to blaspheme. "Women fell down in convulsions; strong men were smitten suddenly to the earth; the preacher was interrupted by bursts of hysteric laughter or hysteric sobbing." Very foolish and absurd, no doubt, sniggered the superior persons of that day. But if Mr. Lecky and other observers may be believed, it was that foolishness of the Methodist Revival that saved the children of these superior persons from having their heads sheared off by an outburst of revolutionary frenzy similar to that of the Reign of Terror.

About the same time that Wesley was preaching in England a great Revival broke out in Wales, of which one of the outward and visible signs most plainly perceptible amongst us today is the fact of the Welsh revolt against the Education Act. That the Liberal party commands today a solid majority among the Welsh members is the direct result of the Revival of 1759, which is associated with the name of Howell Harris, a layman of the Church of England, who, while taking part in the Litany in his parish church, became suddenly filled with a fervent zeal, and went forth to preach the Gospel to his fellowmen. At first the movement was within the pale of the Church. Ten beneficed clergymen were among the Revivalists of that day. What would have happened if the Anglican authorities had possessed the wisdom of the serpent and had followed the example of the Church of Rome in utilizing the zeal of her enthusiasts to extend her own borders, who can say? But the problem never arose. The Anglican Church, true to its evil traditions, cast out the Revivalists, and Welsh Nonconformity was born. Modem Wales is the direct product of the Revival of the eighteenth century.

As a leading Baptist minister said, writing on this subject on November 19th:

The Nonconformist bodies of Wales owe their origin to Religious Revivals, two to that of the seventeenth century and two to that of the eighteenth century. Wales has to thank her past Revivals for the greater part of the energy exhibited in her national, political, and social life. In the Revivals with which the people of Wales have been blessed of God, His Spirit engraved upon the conscience of the nation the terribly solemn truths of existence and the things which belong unto her peace. This gave to her men of Conviction and of courage, and taught her to aspire to all that is good and noble, and whatever her achievements are religiously and socially, they are due mainly to the stimulus received during periods of outpouring of the Spirit of God.

In the nineteenth century the Tractarian Movement may be regarded by some as a Revival. But it was neither preceded by great apathy nor followed by vigorous political progress. The most notable Revival of the century was that which broke out in the United States in the latter end of the fifties, and which spread in a few years over Ulster and Wales, and from thence made its way into England and Scotland. The Revival seems to travel in the opposite direction to the sun. The great Revival of 1740, under Jonathan Edwards in New England, preceded by many years the Welsh Revival under Howell Harris and the English Revival under Wesley and Whitefield. In like manner the Revival that touched Wales in 1859 and England in the early sixties had its birth in 1857 or 1858 across the Atlantic, where it was the direct precursor of the great civil war and the emancipation of the slaves. The Revival of 1859 to 1861 coincided with the closing years of Whig domination, and was followed very speedily by a great movement of popular reform. There was no direct connection between the establishment of household suffrage and the penitent forms and prayer meetings of 1859 and 1861. "*Post hoc*" is not "*propter hoc*". But when Reform follows Revival, the plain man may be pardoned if he sees some connection between the two other than mere coincidence. The coincidence, if it be such, is surely very remarkable The record of Revivals in English history runs thus:

	Revival	Result
12 Century	The Cistercian	Magna Charta
13th	The Friars	Parlamentary Government
14th	Wycliffe	The Peasant Revolt
16th	Tyndale	The Protestant Reformation
17th	Puritanism	The fall of despotism and the founding of New England
17th 1/2	Quakerism	The Revolution of 1688 and the founding of Pennsylvania
18th	Methodist	The Era of Reform
19th	American	The Era of Democracy
20th	Welsh	Who can say?

To the observer of the phenomena of national growth and the evolution of society these periodical Revivals of Religion are as marked a phenomenon in the history of England, possibly of other lands, as the processions of the seasons. To appreciate the prophetic significance of a religious Revival does not necessarily involve any acceptance of the truth of the religion. All that we have to recognize is that the history of human progress in this country has always followed a certain course, which in its main features is as invariable as the great changes which make up our year. Always there is the winter of corruption, of luxury, of indolence, of vice, during which the nation seems to have forgotten God, and to have given itself up to drunkenness, gambling, avarice, and impurity. Men's hearts fail them for fear, and the love of many grows cold. It is the season when, through most of the day, the sun withholds his beams, and a bitter frost chills all the nobler aspirations of the soul. Through such a period of eclipse we have been passing during the last few years. But as the rainbow in the ancient story stands eternal in the heavens as a proof that summer and winter, seed time and harvest, shall fail not, so after such periods of black and bitter wintry reaction always comes the gracious spring-tide with healing in its wings.

And, as we have seen, the outward and visible sign of the coming of spring in the history of the nation is a great revival of religious earnestness - a sudden and widespread outburst of evangelistic fervor. We may dislike many of its manifestations, as we dislike the winds of March or the showers of April, but they occur in almost identical fashion century after century. The form changes. The preaching of the Friars was not exactly the same as the preaching of the Methodists. Wycliffe's Poor Preachers and the Early Friends differed both in dialect and in doctrine. But at bottom all the English Revivals have been identical. One and all represent the spring-time of faith in the heart of man, a sudden rediscovery that life is given him not to please his senses, but to serve his Maker, and that time is but the vestibule of Eternity. The sense of the reality of an ever-living God within, around, above, beneath, in whom we live and move and have our being, and the related sense of a never-dying soul, whose destiny throughout numberless æons of the future years will be influenced by the way in which each day of our mortal probation is spent - these two great truths are rediscovered afresh by the English people every century. The truths blossom in the national heart at these times of spiritual spring-tide as the hawthorn blossoms on the hedge in the merry month of May.

That the Revival time passes is true. So passes spring-tide with its flowers. But as spring is followed by summer, so the Revival of Religion in this country has ever been followed by the summer of reform and the harvest of garnered fruit. It is this which ought to make every thoughtful person of all creeds, or of no creed, watch with the keenest interest the symptoms which indicate the coming of a National Revival. Until this nation goes to the penitent form, it never really pulls itself together for any serious work.

Chapter 3
What I Saw in Wales

The first notice of the existence of the Revival that appeared in the press was published on Nov. 7th, 1904. It was not until Dec. 10th that I went down to Cardiff, and was joined there by the Rev. Thomas Law, the Organizing Secretary of the National Council, and Gipsy Smith, the Evangelist, whom I had not seen since I bade him farewell at Cape Town. On Sunday we went over to the mining village of Mardy and attended three services at which Mr. Evan Roberts was present. I returned to Cardiff that evening and came on to London next morning.

As I wrote out before leaving Cardiff my report for *The Daily Chronicle*, where it appeared on December 13th, was interviewed early on Tuesday morning for *The Methodist Times* of December 15th, and wrote on Tuesday afternoon a report for *The Christian World* of December 15th, I cannot do better than reprint here these first clear impressions of what I found going on in South Wales. I will quote the interview first because it brings out more abruptly and vividly what seems to me the supernatural side of the Revival.

Interview in "The Methodist Times,"
December 15th.

"Well, Mr. Stead, you've been to the Revival. What do you think of it?"

"Sir," said Mr. Stead, "the question is not what I think of it, but what it thinks of me, of yon, and all the rest of us. For it is a very real thing, this Revival: a live thing which seems to have a power and a grip which may get hold of a good many of us who at present are mere spectators."

"Do you think it is on the march, then?"

"A Revival is something like a revolution. It is apt to be wonderfully catching. But you can never say. Look at the way the revolutionary tempest swept over Europe in 1848. But since then revolutions have not spread much beyond the border of the state in which they break out. We may have become immune to Revivals, gospel-hardened or totally indifferent. I don't think so. But I would not like to prophesy."

"But in South Wales the Revival is moving?"

"It reminded me, said Mr. Stead, of the effect which travellers say is produced on the desert by the winds which propel the sand storms, beneath which whole caravans have been engulfed. The wind springs up, no one knows from whence. Its eddying gusts lick up the sands, and soon the whole desert is filled with moving columns of sand, swaying and dancing and whirling as if they were instinct with life. Woe be to the unprotected traveller whose path the sand storm traverses."

"Then do you feel that we are in the track of the storm?"

"Can our people sing? that is the question to be answered before you can decide that. Hitherto the Revival has not strayed beyond the track of the singing people. It has followed the line of song, not of preaching. It has sung its way from one end of South Wales to the other. But, then, the Welsh are a nation of singing birds."

"You speak as if you dreaded the Revival coming your way?"

"No, that is not so. Dread is not the right word. Awe expresses my sentiment better. For you are in the presence of the unknown. I tell you it is a live thing this Revival, and if it gets hold of the people in London, for instance, it will make a pretty considerable shaking up."

"But surely it will be all to the good?"

"Yes, for the good or for those who are all good."

"But what about those who are not good, or who, like the most of us, are a pretty mixed lot? Henry Ward Beecher used to say that if God were to answer the Lord's Prayer and cause His will to be done in earth as it is in heaven, there were streets in New York which would be wrecked as if they had been struck by a tornado. Of course, it may be all to the good that we should be all shaken up; and tornadoes clear the air, and earthquakes are wholesome, but they are not particularly welcome to those who are at ease in Zion."

"Sandstorms in the desert, tornadoes, earthquakes! Really Mr. Stead, your metaphors would imply that your experiences in South Wales have been pretty bad?"

"No," said Mr. Stead. "Not bad at all. Do you remember what the little Quaker child said, when the Scottish express rushed at full speed through the station on the platform on which he was standing? "Were you not frightened, my boy?" said his father. "Oh, no," said the little chap, "a feeling of sweet peace stole into my mind." I felt like that rather. But the thing is awesome. You don't believe in ghosts?"

"Not much. I'll believe them when I see one."

"Well, you have read ghost stories, and can imagine what you would feel if you were alone at midnight in the haunted chamber of some old castle, and you heard slow and stealthy steps stealing along the corridor where the visitant from the other world was said to walk. If you go to South Wales and watch the Revival you will feel pretty much like that. There is something there from the Other World. You cannot say whence it came or whither it was going, but it moves and lives and reaches for you all the time. You see men and women go down in sobbing agony before your eyes as the invisible Hand clutches at their heart. And you shudder. It's pretty grim, I tell you. If you are afraid of strong emotions you'd better give the Revival a wide berth."

"But is it all emotion? Is there no teaching?"

"Precious little. Do you think that teaching is what people want in a Revival? These people, all the people in a land like ours, are taught to death, preached to insensibility. They all know the essential truths. They know that they are not living as they ought to live, and no amount of teaching will add anything to that conviction. To hear some people talk you would imagine that the best way to get a sluggard out of bed is to send a tract on astronomy showing him that according to the fixed and eternal law the sun will rise at a certain hour in the morning. The sluggard does not deny it. He is entirely convinced of it. But what he knows is that it is precious cold at sunrise on a winter's morning, and it is very snug and warm between the blankets. What the sluggard needs is to be well shaken, and in case of need to be pulled out of bed. Roused, the Revival calls it. And the Revival is a rouser rather than a teacher. And that is why I think those Churches which want to go on dozing in the ancient ways had better hold a special series of prayer meetings that the Revival may be prevented coming their way."

"Then I take it that your net impressions were favorable?"

"How could they be otherwise? Did I not feel the pull of that unseen Hand?" And have I not heard the glad outburst of melody that hailed the confession of some who in very truth had found salvation? There is a wonderful spontaneity about it all, and so far its fruits have been good, and only good."

"Will it last?"

"Nothing lasts forever in this mutable world, and the Revival will no more last than the blossom lasted in the field in springtime. But if the blossom had not come and gone there would be no bread in the world today. And as it is with the bread which Mr. Chamberlain would tax, so it is with that other bread which is the harvest that will be gathered in long after this Revival has taken its place in history. But if the analogy of all previous Revivals holds good, this religious awakening will be influencing for good the lives of numberless men and women who will be living and toiling and carrying on the work of this God's world of ours long after you and I have been gathered to our fathers."

The report which I wrote for the Christian World was written for people inside the Churches, who might naturally be supposed to be interested in the reality of the spiritual side of the Revival.

From "The Christian World,"
December 15th.

Will the Revival in South Wales be like a bonfire on ice? Or will it set the heather afire, kindling a blaze which no man can extinguish? The answer is that no one can prophesy confidently as to what the future may bring to us, excepting that it will always both disappoint and exceed our expectations. The Revival in Wales will, in some places, be like a bonfire on ice, which speedily expires for lack of fuel, and yet in other places it may set the heather on fire and produce quite incalculable results.

I cannot profess to have made any exhaustive study of the Revival. Until last Saturday I had only followed it in the newspapers. But from Saturday night till Monday morning I employed every available moment in observing it and in interviewing those who had been in it from the first. I was accompanied throughout the whole of my brief tour by two men who have had as much experience of mission work of a Revivalist nature as anyone outside the Salvation Army. One of them, Gipsy Smith, had come over the same day as I did on the same errand. The other, the Rev. Thomas Law, Organizing Secretary of the Free Church Federation, has been in Wales for some time, and had excellent opportunities of studying the question in various districts in South Wales. I think I am justified in saying that both Mr. Law and Gipsy Smith are absolutely at one with me in the conclusions which I embodied in my report to the Daily Chronicle of Tuesday. During my stay in Wales I had the advantage of hearing the opinions of Principal Edwards and of Commissioner Nicol, of the Salvation

Army, and of several other ministers who have been actively engaged in Christian service in the districts where the Revival has taken place. After my return I had a long consultation with Mr. Bramwell Booth, who knows the district well, and who had visited Cardiff on Saturday, where he met members of his staff from all parts of South Wales, for the express purpose of ascertaining on the spot what was the exact significance of the Revival. I also saw the special emissary dispatched by the Rev. F. B. Meyer for the purpose of spying out the land, and heard from him the impression produced on his mind by what he had seen and heard. The reports in the two local newspapers, which occasionally fill five columns and always fill two or three, also supplied additional confirmatory evidence as to the grip which the movement has taken on the Welsh. I attended three protracted meetings on the Sunday, and I had an hour with Mr. Evan Roberts. I am careful to particularize all my sources of information in order that my readers may know exactly what data I have to go upon in drawing up this report for the readers of the Christian World. My own experience may be of the slightest, and my visit was wonderfully brief. But I think that I may claim that there are few Free Churchmen in the United Kingdom who would not admit that I could not possibly have had more expert advisers or dispassionate witnesses than the persons whom I have named. Nor do I think that any one of them would demur in the least to any statement of fact or broad deduction from the facts which will be found in this article. Had time permitted I would have gladly submitted my report to each and all of them in proofs, nor do I think that they would have made any material alteration.

This being so, I take it that the Christian Churches in England may accept it as now being absolutely beyond all serious dispute that the Revival in South Wales is a very real and a very genuine thing. That there may have been here and there instances of un-wisdom and of extravagance is possible. They have been very few and unimportant. The Welsh are an emotional race, and they are apt to demonstrate their feelings more effusively than phlegmatic Saxons. But I certainly saw nothing of that kind that might not be paralleled in mission services in England. The fact is, there has been so little handle given to the enemy whoever is hungering for occasion to blaspheme, that the Revival, so far, lacks that one great testimony in its favor which all good causes have in the furious abuse of those who may compendiously and picturesquely be described as the staff officers of the devil. Woe be unto you when all men speak well of you was true of Revivals as of anything else. The Revival has, so far, had little of that cause for rejoicing that is supplied by persecution and abuse. The testimony in its favor is almost wearisomely monotonous. Magistrates and policemen, journalists and employers of labor, Salvationists and ordained ministers, all say the same thing, to wit, that the Revival is working mightily for good wherever it has broken out.

Of course, the Doubting Thomases of the land will shake their sceptical heads, and, when convinced against their will that the Revival is bearing good fruit, will ask whether it will last. To which I do not hesitate to reply that some of its fruits will last as long as the human soul endures. That a good deal of the seed which, having fallen on stony ground, has sprung up speedily will presently wither away is a matter of course. It was so when the Parable of the Sower was spoken, it is so today. But the cavillers forget that it is a better thing for seed to spring up, even if it does wither, than for it never to spring up at all. Even if the farmer does not get the full corn in the ear, the green stalk with its succulent leaves will make capital fodder for his stock. Most of the seed sown at times when we hear of no showers of blessings to fertilize the soil never springs up at all. Little as the cavillers about the evanescent nature of Revivals realize it, they are appealing to one of the most antiquated notions of a narrow orthodoxy. Those who imagine that the only object of the Christian Gospel is to save a man's soul from the everlasting burnings may reasonably object that a Revival is of no good if, after having roused the sinner, it does not keep him soundly saved until the hour and article of death. It is in that case very much like taking out an insurance policy and letting it lapse by forgetting to pay the premiums regularly till death. But there are very few who regard conversion as an insurance policy against hell fire. Hence every single day or week or month or year is all to the good. It is, of course, best of all when a consecrated life is crowned by a triumphant death. But it is not a bad thing - on the contrary, it is a very good thing - to raise human lives to a higher moral level for a comparatively short period, even if after that time they all slide back. It is better to have lived well for a year than never to have been above the mire at all. As a matter of fact, most of the best men of the older generation in Wales today were brought in when quite youths in the great Revival of 1859.

So far as I could discover, the movement is in very good hands - so far as it is in any hands at all save those of the invisible Spirit to which all the Revivalists constantly appeal. Never was there a religious movement so little indebted to the guiding brain of its leaders. It seems to be going on its own. There is no commanding human genius inspiring the advance. Ministers, each in their own churches, open the meetings. But when once they are started they obey the Spirit. It reminds one of the Quakers in more ways than one. In the seventeenth century the Friends were the Revivalists of the time. With the exception of the singing, they would feel themselves thoroughly at home in South Wales today. In most missions tune is everything. In South Wales the leading rôle is taken by the third Person of the Trinity. So jealous are they of quenching the Spirit that the Tory daily payer - just think of it - the organ of the Established Church and ease and order and all the rest of the conventions - actually fumed and fretted because at one meeting some persons who were giving unbridled rein to their spiritual impulses, to the annoyance of the whole congregation, were asked to restrain their exuberance of their demonstrations! If this thing goes on we shall see the Times and the

Guardian reproving General Booth for endeavoring to repress the excesses of excitement at all-night meetings.

I have said that the early Friends would be at home in the Welsh valleys with the exception of the singing. It is a great exception. For the special note of the Revival is that the gospel message is being sung rather than preached. And such singing! The whole congregation sing - as if they were making melody in their hearts to the Lord. The sermon is a poor thing compared with the Psalm and hymn and spiritual song. The Welsh have hymns of their own, which were strange to me. I have no musical ear, but the rhythm and the cadence of some of these Welsh tunes linger in my memory as the murmur of the wave in the convolutions of the shell. There is one beginning with the Welsh equivalent for Holy breezes, which was a great favorite; and so is another which gives thanks to the all merciful God for remembering us poor creatures who are as the dust of the earth. But most of the hymns were the old familiar hymns of every mission service. Occasionally they sang "Lead, kindly Light", but much more frequently "Jesus, Lover of my soul", "I need Thee every hour", "Lord, I hear of showers of blessings", all in Welsh, of course, although very often, after singing the chorus over and over again in Welsh, they would sing it once or twice in English. Among the solos there was Mr. Sankey's "Ninety and nine", which, although turned out of the revised Methodist Hymn Book, is written on the hearts of the Welsh. "Jesus of Nazareth passes by" is another favorite solo. The only new song taken over from the Torrey and Alexander Mission was sung over and over again:

"Tell mother I'll be there
In answer to her prayer,
This message, blessed Savior, to her bear.
Tell mother I'll be there,
Heavens joys with her to share,
Oh, tell my darling mother I'll be there."

In the Gospel the Prodigal Son comes back to his father. It is perhaps an indication of the swing of the slow pendulum back to the days of the matriarchate that in Wales today the father takes a back seat. It is the mother who is always to the front.

Nor is that the only welcome indication of the toppling of the hateful and unchristian ascendancy of the male. The old objection of many of the Welsh Churches to the equal ministry of women has gone by the board. The Singing Sisters who surround Mr. Evan Roberts are as indispensable as Mr. Sankey was to Mr. Moody. Women pray, sing, testify, and speak as freely as men - no one daring to make them afraid. The Salvation Army has not labored in vain.

There is no inquiry room, no penitent form. The wrestle with unbelief, the combat with the evil one for the soul of the convicted sinner, goes on in the midst of the people. It is all intensely dramatic. Sometimes unspeakably tragic. At other times full of exultant triumph. Mr. Evan Roberts, towards the close of the meeting, asks all who from their hearts believe and confess their Savior to rise. At the meetings at which I was present nearly everybody was standing. Then for the sitting remnant the storm of prayer rises to the mercy seat. When one after another rises to his feet, glad strains of jubilant song burst from the watching multitude. No one has a hymn book; no one gives out a hymn. The congregation seems moved by a simultaneous impulse. It is all very wonderful, sometimes almost eerie in its suggestiveness of the presence of Another Whom no eye can see, but Who moves on the wings of the wind.

Who can say to what this thing may not grow? Who can put bounds to the flood of awakened enthusiasm? One thing is certain - no one could wish to erect a barrier save those who do not love their fellowmen.

The report, which I wrote for the Daily chronicle was written for the general public, who are comparatively indifferent to the spiritual side of the Revival, but who regard its social and psychological aspects with a mild degree of interest.

From "The Daily Chronicle"
December 13th.

As springtime precedes summer, and seedtime harvest, so every great onward step in the social and political progress of Great Britain has ever been preceded by a national Revival of Religion. The sequence is as unmistakable as it is invariable. It was as constant when England was Catholic as it has been since the Reformation.

Hence it is not necessary to be Evangelical, Christian, or even religious, to regard with keen interest every stirring of popular enthusiasm that takes the familiar form of a Revival. Men may despise it, hate it, or fear it, but there is no mistaking its significance. It is the precursor of progress, the herald of advance. It may be as evanescent as the blossom of the orchard, but without it there would be no fruit.

The question, therefore, which I set out to South Wales to discuss with those who are in the midst of what is called the Welsh Revival was whether this popular stir and widespread awakening might be regarded as the forerunner of a great national - nay, possibly of a still wider - movement, which might bring in its wake social and political changes profoundly improving the condition of the human race. The net conclusion at which I have arrived after twenty-four hours spent in the heart of it is that, while no one can dogmatize and no one can prophesy, it would be advisable for the wide-awake journalists to drop the newspaper headline, "The Welsh Revival", and describe it in future as "The Rising Revival in the West".

Nor would I like to venture to predict how long or how short a time it will be before that heading in its turn will have to give way to the simple title of "The Revival", which will be neither in the west alone, nor in the east, but which will spread over the whole land as the waters cover the face of the mighty deep. Of course, the signs of the times may be misleading, and that which seems most probable may never happen. But writing today in the midst of it all, I would say with all earnestness, Look out!

The British Empire, as Admiral Fisher is never tired of repeating, floats upon the British Navy. But the British Navy steams on Welsh coal. The driving force of all our battleships is hewn from the mines of these Welsh valleys by the men amongst whom this remarkable religious awakening has taken place. On Sunday morning, as the slow train crawled down the gloomy valleys. - for there was the mirk of coming snow in the air, and there was no sun in the sky - I could not avoid the obvious and insistent suggestion of the thought that Welsh religious enthusiasm may be destined to impart as compelling an impulse to the Churches of the world as Welsh coal supplies to its navies.

Nor was the force of the suggestion weakened when, after attending three prolonged services at Mardy, a village of 5,000 inhabitants, lying on the other side of Pontypridd, I found the flame of Welsh religious enthusiasm as smokeless as its coal. There are no advertisements, no brass bands, no posters, no huge tents. All the paraphernalia of the got-up job are conspicuous by their absence.

Neither is there any organization, nor is there a director, at least none that is visible to the human eye. In the crowded chapels they even dispense with instrumental music. On Sunday night no note issued from the organ pipes. There was no need of instruments, for in and around and above and. beneath surged the all-pervading thrill and throb of a multitude praying, and singing as they prayed.

The vast congregations were as soberly sane, as orderly, and at least as reverent as any congregation I ever saw beneath the dome of St. Paul's, when I used to go to hear Canon Liddon, the Chrysostom of the English pulpit. But it was aflame with a passionate religious enthusiasm, the like of which I have never seen in St. Paul's. Tier above tier, from the crowded aisles to the loftiest gallery, sat or stood, as necessity dictated, eager hundreds of serious men and thoughtful women, their eyes riveted upon the platform or upon whatever other part of the building was the storm center of the meeting.

There was absolutely nothing wild, violent, hysterical, unless it be hysterical for the laboring breast to heave with sobbing that cannot be repressed, and the throat to choke with emotion as a sense of the awful horror and shame of a wasted life suddenly bursts upon the soul. On all sides there was the solemn gladness of men and women upon whose eyes has dawned the splendor of a new day, the foretaste of whose glories they are enjoying in the quickened sense of human fellowship and a keen glad zest added to their own lives.

The most thorough-going materialist who resolutely and forever rejects as inconceivable the existence of the soul in man, and to whom the universe is but the infinite empty eye-socket of a dead God, could not fail to be impressed by the pathetic sincerity of these men nor, if he were just, could he refuse to recognize that out of their faith in the creed which he has rejected they have drawn, and are drawing, a motive power that makes for righteousness, and not only for righteousness, but for the joy of living, that he would be powerless to give them.

Employers tell me that the quality of the work the miners are putting in has improved. Waste is less, men go to their daily toil with a new spirit of gladness in their labor. In the long dim galleries of the mine, where once the haulers swore at their ponies in Welshified English terms of blasphemy, there is now but to be heard the haunting melody of the Revival music. The pit ponies, like the American mules, having been driven by oaths and curses since they first bore the yoke, are being retrained to do their work without the incentive of profanity.

There is less drinking, less idleness, less gambling. Men record with almost incredulous amazement how one football player after another has foresworn cards and drink and the gladiatorial games, and is living a sober and godly life, putting his energy into the Revival. More wonderful still, and almost incredible to those who know how journalism lives and thrives upon gambling, and how Toryism is broad-based upon the drinking habits of the people, the Tory daily paper of South Wales has devoted its columns day after day to reporting and defending the movement which declares war to the death against both gambling and drink.

How came this strange uplift of the earnestness of a whole community? Who can say? The wind bloweth where it listeth. Some tell you one thing, some another. All agree that it began some few months ago in Cardiganshire, eddied hither and thither, spreading like fire from valley to valley, until, as one observer said to me, Wherever it came from, or however it began, all South Wales today is in a flame.

One report says that the first outward and visible sign that there was a new power and spirit among the people was witnessed at a meeting in a country chapel in Cardiganshire. The preacher, after an earnest appeal to the unconverted, besought those of his hearers whose hearts were moved within them to testify before the congregation their decision to serve the Lord. A long and painful pause followed. Again came the solemn appeal. Again the embarrassing silence.

But it was broken after a pause by the rising of a girl, a young Welsh woman, who with trembling accents spoke up and said, "If no one else will, then I must say that I do love my Lord Jesus Christ with all my heart". The ice was broken. One after another stood up and made public confessions with tears and thanksgiving.

So it began. So it is going on. "If no one else, then I must." It is "Here I am: send me! This public self-consecration, this definite and decisive avowal of a determination to put under their feet their dead past of vice and sin and indifference, and to reach out towards a higher ideal of human existence, is going on everywhere in South Wales. Nor, if we think of it sanely and look at it in the right perspective, is there a nobler spectacle appealing more directly to the highest instincts of our nature to be seen in all the world today.

At Mardy, where I spent Sunday, the miners are voluntarily taxing themselves this year three half-pence in the pound of their weekly wages to build an institute, public hall, library, and reading room. By their express request the money is deducted from their wages on pay-day. They have created a library of 2,000 books, capitally selected and well used. They have about half-a-dozen chapels and churches, a co-operative society, and the usual appliances of civilization. They have every outward and visible sign of industrial prosperity. It is a mining village pure and simple, industrial democracy in its nakedest primitive form.

In this village I attended three meetings on Sunday - two and a half hours in the morning, two and a half hours in the afternoon, and two hours at night, when I had to leave to catch the train. At all these meetings the same kind of thing went on - the same kind of congregations assembled, the same strained, intense emotion was manifest. Aisles were crowded. Pulpit stairs were packed, and - mirabile dictu! - two-thirds of the congregation were men, and at least one-half young men.

"There," said one, "is the hope and the glory of the movement." Here and there is a grey head. But the majority of the congregation were stalwart young miners, who gave the meeting all the fervor and swing and enthusiasm of youth. The Revival had been going on in Mardy for a fortnight. All the churches had been holding services every night with great results, At the Baptist Church they had to report the addition of nearly fifty members, fifty were waiting for baptism, thirty-five backsliders had been reclaimed.

In Mardy the fortnight's services had resulted in five hundred conversions. And this, be it noted, when each place of worship was going on its own. Mr. Evan Roberts, the so-called boy preacher of the Revival, and his singing sisterhood did not reach Mardy until the Sunday of my visit.

I have called Evan Roberts the so-called boy preacher, because he is neither a boy nor a preacher. He is a tall, graceful, good-looking young man of twenty-six, with a pleading eye and a most winsome smile. If he is a boy, he is a six-foot boy, and six-footers are usually past their boyhood. As he is not a boy, neither is he a preacher. He talks simply, unaffectedly, earnestly, now and then, but he makes no sermons, and preaching is emphatically not the note of this Revival in the West. If it has been by the foolishness of preaching men have been saved heretofore, that agency seems as if it were destined to take a back seat in the present movement.

The Revival is borne along upon billowing waves of sacred song. It is to other Revivals what the Italian Opera is to the ordinary theatre. It is the singing, not the preaching, that is the instrument which is most efficacious in striking the hearts of men. In this respect these services in the Welsh chapel reminded me strangely of the beautiful liturgical services of the Greek Church, notably in St. Isaac of St. Petersburg on Easter morn, - and in the receptions of the pilgrim at the Troitski Monastery, near Moscow.

The most extraordinary thing about the meetings which I attended was the extent to which they were absolutely without any human direction or leadership. We must obey the Spirit, is the watchword of Evan Roberts, and he is as obedient as the humblest of his followers. The meetings open - after any amount of preliminary singing, while the congregation is assembling - by the reading of a chapter or a psalm. Then it is go as you please for two hours or more.

And the amazing thing is that it does go and does not get entangled in what might seem to be inevitable confusion. Three-fourths of the meeting consist of singing. No one uses a hymn book. No one gives out a hymn. The last person to control the meeting in any way is Mr. Evan Roberts. People pray and sing, give testimony; exhort as the Spirit moves them. As a study of the psychology of crowds, I have seen nothing like it. You feel that the thousand or fifteen hundred persons before you have become merged into one myriad-headed but single-souled personality.

You can watch what they call the influence of the power of the Spirit playing over the crowded congregation as a eddying wind plays over the surface of a pond. If anyone carried away by his feelings prays too long, or if any one when speaking fails to touch the right note, someone - it may be anybody - commences to sing. For a moment there is a hesitation as if the meeting were in doubt as to its decision, whether to hear the speaker, or to continue to join in the prayer, or whether to sing. If it decides to hear and to pray, the singing dies away. If, on the other hand, as it usually happens, the people decide to sing, the chorus swells in volume until it drowns all other sound.

A very remarkable instance of this abandonment of the meeting to the spontaneous impulse, not merely of those within the walls, but of those crowded outside, who were unable to get in, occurred on Sunday night. Twice the order of proceeding, if order it can be called, was altered by the crowd outside, who, being moved by some mysterious impulse, started a hymn on their own account, which was at once taken up by the congregation within. On one of these occasions Evan Roberts was addressing the meeting. He at once gave way, and the singing became general.

The prayers are largely autobiographical, and some of them intensely dramatic. On one occasion an impassioned and moving appeal to the Deity was accompanied throughout by an exquisitely rendered hymn, sung by three of the Singing Sisters. It was like the undertone of the orchestra when some leading singer is holding the house.

The Singing Sisters - there are five of them, one, Mme. Morgan, who was a professional singer - are as conspicuous figures in the movement as Evan Roberts himself. Some of their solos are wonders of dramatic and musical appeal. Nor is the effect lessened by the fact that the singers, like the speakers, sometimes break down in sobs and tears. The meeting always breaks out into a passionate and consoling song, until the soloist, having recovered her breath, rises from her knees and resumes her song.

The praying and singing are both wonderful, but more impressive than either are the breaks which occur when utterance can no more, and the sobbing in the silence momentarily heard is drowned in a tempest of melody. No need for an organ. The assembly was its own organ as a thousand sorrowing or rejoicing hearts found expression in the sacred psalmody of their native hills.

Repentance, open confession, intercessory prayer, and, above all else, this marvelous musical liturgy - a liturgy unwritten but heartfelt, a mighty chorus rising like the thunder of the surge on a rockbound shore, ever and anon broken by the flute-like note of the Singing Sisters, whose melody was as sweet and as spontaneous as the music of the throstle in the grove or the lark in the sky. And all this vast quivering, throbbing, singing, praying, exultant multitude intensely conscious of the all-pervading influence of some invisible reality - now for the first time moving palpable though not tangible in their midst.

They called it the Spirit of God. Those who have not witnessed it may call it what they will; I am inclined to agree with those on the spot. For man, being, according to the Orthodox, evil, can do no good thing of himself, so, as Cardinal Manning used to say, "Wherever you behold a good thing, there you see the working of the Holy Ghost." And the Revival, as I saw it, was emphatically a good thing.

Chapter 4
Evan Roberts

THE Revival in South Wales is not the work of any one man or of any number of men, but the most conspicuous figure in this strange religious awakening is undoubtedly that of the young Welsh collier-student, Mr. Evan Roberts. Until last November no one had heard of him. Today his name is on every tongue in Wales, and everywhere in all the land people are asking what manner of man this new Evangelist may be.

Mr. Evan Roberts is a tall, graceful young man of twenty-six, who, until last year, was at work as a collier in the Broadoak Colliery, Loughor, a Welsh village near which an express train was wrecked a few months ago, with great loss of life. He is the son of Methodist parents, and attended the Movrah Methodist Chapel in Loughor. Like many Welshmen, he is a poet, and contributed many fine verses to the Golofn Gymraag in *The Cardiff Times* under the name of "Bwlchydd". He was always of a pious disposition, but according to his own account, although he was a Church member and a worker in the Sunday school, he was not a Christian until little more than fifteen months ago. His own words at Trecynon, on November 14th, were as follows:

Some people had said he was a Methodist. He did not know what he was. Sectarianism melted in the fire of the Holy Spirit, and all men who believed became one happy family. For years he was a faithful member of the Church, a zealous worker, and a free giver. But he had recently discovered that he was not a Christian, and there were thousands like him. It was only since he had made that discovery that a new light had come into his life. That same light was shining upon all men if they would but open their eyes and their hearts.

How did he make that discovery? Various accounts have been given of the awakening of Evan Roberts. According to one account, he was present at an address delivered by the Rev. F. B. Meyer at a religious Convention in August, 1903, when a pledge was given by several present, including Roberts, that they would spend a whole day every month praying for a Revival. According to Mr. Roberts's own account, he seems to have been chiefly exercised in his devotions by a melancholy conviction of the failure of Christianity. He was then living at Loughor, working in the mine and spending his leisure in studying for the ministry. He used to take his Bible down the mine, and while at work would put it away in some convenient hole or nook near his working place, ready to his hand when he could snatch a moment or two to scan its beloved pages. A serious explosion occurred one day. The future Welsh Revivalist escaped practical unhurt, but the leaves of his Bible were scorched by the fiery blast.

It was during the latter months of his stay at Loughor, before he went to the preparatory school or college at Newcastle Emlyn, that the light dawned upon him in the privacy of his own room. He seems to have been very fervent in prayer. A Mr. Davies, a Newport Baptist, is the authority for the statement that Roberts was turned out of his lodgings by his landlady, who thought that in his enthusiasm he was possessed or somewhat mad. He spent hours praying and preaching in his rooms, until the lady became afraid of him and asked him to leave. The following narrative I had from his own lips when I met him at tea on Sunday afternoon at Mardy. I asked him - Can you tell me how you began to take to this work?

"Oh, yes, that I will," said Mr. Roberts, "if you wish to hear of it. For a long, long time I was much troubled in my soul and my heart by thinking over the failure of Christianity. Oh! it seemed such a failure - such a failure - and I prayed and prayed, but nothing seemed to give me any relief. But one night, after I had been in great distress praying about this, I went to sleep, and at one o'clock in the morning suddenly I was waked up out of my sleep, and I found myself, with unspeakable joy and awe, in the very presence of the Almighty God. And for the space of four hours I was privileged to speak face to face with Him as a man speaks face to face with a friend. At five o'clock it seemed to me as if I again returned to earth." [1]

[1] Mr. J. Addington Symonds records a somewhat similar experience when under chloroform. He says: I thought that I was near death, when suddenly my soul became aware of God, who was manifestly dealing with me, handling me, so to speak, in an intense personal present reality. I felt Him streaming in like light upon me. I cannot describe the ecstasy I felt. When the effect of the anaesthetic faded, he longed for death, rather than to lose "that long dateless ecstasy of vision" in which he felt "the very God in all purity and tenderness and truth and absolute love." He adds: "The question remains, is it possible that the inner sense of reality which succeeded when my flesh was dead to impressions from without to the ordinary sense of physical relations was not a delusion but an actual experience? Is it possible that I in that moment felt what some of the saints have said they always felt, the undemonstrable but irrefragable certainty of God?" -. Symonds's works, cited by James, p. 392.

See also the experiences of Madame Guyon: "It seemed to me that God came at the precise time and woke me from sleep in order that I might enjoy Him." - *Ib.* p. 277.

"Were you not dreaming?" I asked.

"No, I was wide awake. And it was not only that morning, but every morning for three or four months. Always I enjoyed four hours of that wonderful communion with God. I cannot describe it. I felt it, and it seemed to change all my nature, and I saw things in a different light, and I knew that God was going to work in the land, and not this land only, but in all the world. [2]

[2] This mystic vision, which enables a man to comprehend the secret of God in the creation and ordering of the universe, was common to all the great saints, and also to one not usually classed as a saint, Walt Whitman. George Fox was so confident that the nature and virtues of all things had been opened to him by the Lord that he actually contemplated practicing physic for the good of mankind. Ignatius Loyola, on the steps of the choir of the Dominican church, saw in a distinct manner the plan of Divine Wisdom in the creation of the world. St. Teresa says that it was granted to her one day to perceive in one instant how all things are seen and contained in God. Jacob Boehme, in one quarter of a day in trance, saw and knew the being of all things. Whitman wrote:

"I mind how once we (my soul and I) lay, such a transparent summer morning,
Swiftly arose to spread around me the peace and knowledge
That pass all the argument of the earth;
And I know that the hand of God is the promise of my own;
And I know that the Spirit of God is the brother of my own,
And that all the men ever born are also my brothers, and the women my sisters and lovers,
And that a kelson of the creation is love." - *Ib.*, p. 396.

Excuse me, I said, but, as an old interviewer, may I ask if, when the mystic ecstasy passed, you put on paper all that you remembered of these times of communion?

"No, I wrote nothing at all," [3] said Mr. Roberts. "It went on all the time until I had to go to Newcastle Emlyn to the college to prepare for the ministry. I dreaded to go, for fear I should lose these four hours with God every morning. But I had to go, and it happened as I feared. For a whole month He came no more, and I was in darkness. And my heart became as a stone. Even the sight of the Cross brought no tears to my eyes. So it continued until, to my great joy, He returned to me, and I had again the glorious communion. And He said I must go and speak to my people in my own village. But I did not go. I did not feel as if I could go to speak to my own people."

[3] Professor James writing on the mystical absorption of the Sufis into God says: "The incommunicableness of the transport is the keynote of all mysticism. Mystical truth exists for the individual who has the transport, but for no one else. – *Symond's works, etc.*, p. 404.

"May I ask," I said, "if He of whom you speak appeared to you as Jesus Christ?"

"No," said Mr. Roberts, "not so; it was the personal God, not as Jesus."

"As God the Father Almighty?" I said.

"Yes," said Mr. Roberts, "and the Holy Spirit." [4]

[4] George Fox used to converse with Jesus Christ; but St. Teresa, like Evan Roberts, spoke with God. She says: "God establishes Himself in the interior of the soul in such a way that when she returns to herself it is wholly impossible for her to doubt that she has been in God and God in her. This truth remained so strongly impressed on her that even though many years should pass without the condition returning, she can neither forget the favor she received nor doubt of the reality." - *Symond's works, etc.*, p. 409.

"Pardon me," I said, "but I interrupted you. Pray go on."

"I did not go to my people, but I was troubled and ill at ease. And one Sunday, as I sat in the chapel, I could not fix my mind upon the service, for always before my eyes I saw, as in a vision, the schoolroom in my own village. And there, sitting in rows before me, I saw my old companions and all the young people, and I saw myself addressing them. I shook my head impatiently, and strove to drive away this vision, but it always came back. And I heard a voice in my inward ear as plain as anything, saying, "Go and speak to these people." And for a long time I would not. But the pressure became greater and greater, and I could hear nothing of the sermon. Then at last I could resist no longer, and I said, "Well, Lord, if it is Thy will, I will go." Then instantly the vision vanished, and the whole chapel became filled with light so dazzling that I could faintly see the minister in the pulpit, and between him and me the glory as the light of the sun in heaven." [5]

[5] This, again, is one of the most familiar phenomena of ecstasy. Professor James says: There is one form of sensory automatism which possibly deserves special notice on account of its frequency. I refer to hallucinatory or pseudo-hallucinatory luminous phenomena, photisms, to use the term of the psychologists. St. Paul's blinding heavenly vision seems to have been a phenomenon of this order. So does Constantine's Cross in the sky. Col. Gardner sees a blazing light. Finney says, "A light perfectly ineffable shone in my soul." - *Symond's works, etc.*, p. 252.

"And then you went home?"

No; I went to my tutor, and told him all things, and asked him if he believed that it was of God or of the devil? And he said the devil does not put good thoughts into the mind. I must go and obey the heavenly vision. So I went back to my own village, and I saw my own minister, and him also I told. And he said that I might try and see what I could do, but that the ground was stony, and the task would be hard.

Did you find it so?

I asked the young people to come together, for I wanted to talk to them. They came, and I stood up to talk to them, and, behold, it was even as I had seen it in the church at Newcastle Emlyn. The young people sat as I had seen them sitting, altogether in rows before me, and I was speaking to them even as it had been shown to me. At first they did not seem inclined to listen; but I went on, and at last the power of the Spirit came down, and six came out for Jesus. But I was not satisfied. "Oh, Lord," I said, "give me six more - I must have six more!" And we prayed together. At last the seventh came, and then the eighth and the ninth together, and after a time the tenth, and then the eleventh, and last of all came the twelfth also. But no more. And they saw that the Lord had given me the second six, and they began to believe in the power of prayer."

"Then after that you went on?"

"First I tried to speak to some other young people in another church, and asked them to come. But the news had gone out, and the old people said, May we not come too? And I could not refuse them. So they came, and they kept on coming now here, now there all the time, and I have never had time to go back to college."

Not much chance, indeed, at present. Three meetings every day, lasting, with breaks for meals, from ten a.m. till twelve p.m., and sometimes later, leave scant leisure for studying elsewhere than in the hearts and souls of men. If only his body will hold out, and his nervous system does not give way, he will have time to study hereafter. At present he has other work in hand.

The story that is told in the papers pieces out Mr. Roberts's own narrative. According to the Rev. Seth Joshua, a mission from the New Quay Christian Endeavour Society came to Newcastle Emlyn, and it was at one of their meetings that Evan Roberts first showed his marvelous power in prayer.

Whatever truth there may be in this link in the chain, there is no doubt that Mr. Evan Roberts began to preach and to pray at the Movrah Methodist Church in Loughor about the beginning of November. The most extraordinary results followed. The whole community was shaken. Meetings were kept up till half-past four, and then at six the villagers would be wakened by the tramp of the crowds going to the early morning prayer meetings. His energy seemed inexhaustible. In those early days, said a writer in *The South Wales Daily News* (November 14th):

Roberts does not call his hearers to repentance, but speaks of having been called to fulfil the words of the prophet Joel. "Your old men shall dream dreams; your young men shall see visions." He tells the audience that he is speaking under the influence of the Holy Spirit, and he describes what he sees, and it strikes some of the congregation that he is unfathoming unconsciously some of the mysteries of the Book of Revelation. His words have a remarkable effect. He does not speak much, but invites the congregation to sing, or pray, or read the Scripture as the Spirit moves them.

Mr. Roberts frequently describes visions that had appeared to him at prayer. For instance:

He said that when he was before the throne of grace he saw appearing before him a key. He did not understand the meaning of this sign. Just then, however, three members of the congregation rose to their feet and said that they had been converted. "My vision is explained," said Mr. Roberts, ecstatically; "it was the key by which God opened your hearts."

On another occasion he reverted to his experiences at Newcastle Emlyn, and told them of another vision. He said (South Wales Daily News, November 19th):

It was a few Sundays ago at Newcastle Emlyn. For days he had been brooding over the apparent failure of modem Christian agencies; and he felt wounded in the spirit that the Church of God should so often be attacked. While in this Slough of Despond he walked in the garden. It was about four p.m. Suddenly, in the hedge on his left, he saw a face full of scorn, hatred, and derision, and heard a laugh as of defiance. It was the Prince of this World, who exulted in his despondency. Then there suddenly appeared another figure, gloriously arrayed in white, bearing in hand a flaming sword borne aloft. The sword fell athwart the first figure, and it instantly disappeared. He could not see the face of the sword-bearer. "Do you not see the moral?" queried the missioner, with face beaming with delight. "Is it not that the Church of Christ is to be triumphant?"

Significant glances passed between many people in the congregation. Visions? What does the man mean? He is speaking in parables. So far he has been a sane speaker, and with no trace about him of the fanatic. He cannot mean to convey that ---. But we are speedily undeceived. "I told the Rev. Evan Phillips of what I had seen, and he answered me that in the state of despondency I was in I might easily have imagined the vision. But" --- with strong emphasis --- "I know what I saw. It was a distinct vision. There was no mistake. And, full of the promise which that vision conveyed, I went to Loughor, and from Loughor to Aberdare, and from Aberdare to Pontycymmer. And what do I see? The promise literally fulfilled. The sword is descending on all hands, and Satan is put to flight. Amen."

It has been said that Mr. Roberts never preaches. He does, however, or rather he did at the beginning of his career deliver long addresses, which were simple, direct Gospel appeals. Joyousness was the note of all his discourse, the joyousness of a junior partner conscious that his Senior is with him and is entrusting him with a most responsible mission.

He exclaimed once: "Oh, if you only saw Christ, you would love Him. How can I repay Him for the privilege of going through Wales to proclaim His love?"

At Pyle, November 21st, speaking of the work that is being done, Mr. Roberts joyously clapped his hands and shouted, "Aha, aha," but remarked that this sort of thing could not go on forever - this fever-heat could not be kept going long; but let them keep it going as long as they could; let them keep it going with a swing (which he illustrated with a swing of his right arm), to raise the Churches to a higher level, and then they could settle down to business. At the end of November he gave it as his conviction that 100,000 souls would be won before the end of the Revival in Wales. In December he said: "At one time I said I would be satisfied with 100,000 converts and then would be willing to die, but now I want the whole world."

Again he says: "Isn't it all wonderful how the Spirit responds? It is not me - it is the Spirit, the Spirit."

To describe the address that follows as a sermon would be a misnomer. He is buoyant, joyous, almost bubbling over with merriment. It is "the joy of Christ," he explains, "and you can laugh - yes, laugh out of sheer joy at the Throne of Grace."

Yet he always shrinks modestly from claiming any of the results that follow his mission; sometimes he declines to let his movements be announced. "People must not rely upon me." This is his constant cry. "I have nothing for them. They must rely upon Him who alone can minister to their needs."

When I talked with him, he said:

"The movement is not of me, it is of God. I would not dare to try to direct it. Obey the Spirit, that is our word in everything. It is the Spirit alone which is leading us in our meetings and in all that is done."

"You do not preach, or teach, or control the meetings?"

"Why should I teach when the Spirit is teaching? What need have these people to be told that they are Sinners? What they need is salvation. Do they not know it? It is not knowledge that they lack, but decision - action. And why should I control the meetings? The meetings control themselves, or rather the Spirit that is in them controls them."

"You find the ministry of the Singing sisters useful?"

"Most useful. They go with me wherever I go. I never part from them without feeling that something is absent if they are not there. The Singing is very important, but not everything. No. The public confession is also important - more SO than the speaking. True, I talk to them a little. But the meetings go of themselves."

"Do you propose to go to England?"

"No. To North Wales next. They say North Wales is Stony cold, but I believe the Holy Spirit will work there also. Oh, yes, God will move North Wales also."

All his movements are governed by the answers he receives to prayer. "Will you go to Cardiff?" they asked him. He paused, and then replied in the negative, the answer to his thought-prayer having been almost instantaneous. He usually speaks in Welsh, but he can speak English, although not with the beauty and polish of his native tongue. The newspapers publish translated scraps rather than reports of his remarks. Here are a few sentences:

"Whilst sect was fighting against sect the devil was clapping his hands with glee, and encouraging the fight. Let all people be one, with one object - the salvation of sinners. Men refused to accept the Gospel and confess because, they said, of the gloom and uncertainty of the future. They looked to the future without having opened their eyes to the infinite glories of the present."

"All must obey, he declares, all must work. There is no room in the Church for idlers. Are you an idler? Then your place is outside. Be as simple in your worshipping as possible, the simpler the better, There is no need to shout, he went on, and no one need be ashamed to confess Christ."

He dwells sometimes on the sufferings of Christ until he falls prone, sobs choking his utterance. While absolutely tolerant of all manifestations of the Spirit, he is stern to check any disorder. At Ferndale, where some persons had been disturbing the meeting by exuberant and unseemly noises, he said: "He who would walk with God must come to His house in a spirit of prayer, of humility, of awe. Joy is permissible in the house, but it must be sanctified joy. For think of the majesty of the Divine Person. Father --- yes, a Father truly, but we must be even as little children, in humility, remembering that we are sinners. We can, we are taught to entreat for the descent of the Spirit, but beware lest the entreaty becomes a rude, imperious command. If we truly walk with God, there can be no disorder, no indecency."

On another occasion he pleaded for a Service of Silence, to convince the world that the power at work in those gatherings was the power of the Holy Spirit, not that of man. "Let us have five minutes of absolutely silent prayers" -- an effective reversion to the practice of the Society of Friends.

His method of conducting a meeting is to allow it to conduct itself. But he usually contrives to expound his four principles, and to summon his hearers to make public confession.

The following is the best report which I have been able to piece together after a diligent study of all the papers published since the Revival began. He addresses his audience thus:

Do you desire an outpouring of the Holy Spirit?

Very well. Four conditions must be observed. They are essential.

(1) Is there any sin in your past life that you have not confessed to God? On your knees at once. Your past must be at peace.

(2) Is there anything in your life that is doubtful? Anything you cannot decide whether it is good or evil? Away with it! There must not be!

(3) Obey the Spirit.

(4) Confess Christ publicly before men.

After the meeting has gone on for some time Roberts proceeds to put his testing questions. I quote the description given by *The South Wales Daily News* on December 14th:

The missioner is now at work. He has three questions to put. He has been told, commanded, imperatively commanded, to put the questions, and he dare not disobey. He could never sleep if he didn't put them.

(1) Will every member of a Christian Church stand up? There is immediate response. Few, very few, are sitting. But a second later we are surprised by the announcement from the gallery that some are standing who are not members. "Come, friends," exclaims the missioner, "have the courage for once to show your side. You will be welcome to come over to our side once you are truly ashamed of your own. Not until then. Let us have no hypocrisy."

(2) "Will all those who love the Lord Jesus Christ stand up? Now, please, be careful. Act conscientiously, lest Gods judgement fall upon you. Those who truly love the Lord Jesus - and they only."

Again a great crowd responds, and to the query, "Do you really and truly love Him?" there comes a loud, triumphant answer,

"Yes."

(3) "Now for the question which Christ put to Peter. It is now put to you individually. Do you love Jesus 'more than these' -- more than all things?"

It's a crucial moment - the query is so startling and unexpected. There is a momentary hesitation, and then once more the congregation is on its feet, and there is a joyful, triumphant rendering of "Diadem."

> Bring forth the royal diadem
> And crown Him Lord of all.

"You have made a great declaration - you love Hun more than all things, all things. We shall presently see how sincere is the declaration. We shall see it in crowded attendances at prayer meetings, at church meetings. We shall see it in the daily study of God's own Book, We shall no longer hear the old excuse, No time to read the Bible. Have you time to eat? The needs of the body are attended to, but, bobol anwyl, what of the sustenance of the soul that is so much more precious? The soul ever thirsts for God. You must be in touch with God's Word every day, every day, were it only one verse."

Have all obeyed the third command to stand up? No, not all. A few are sitting. The test is too severe. "One has gone out," exclaims a voice in the gallery; "he cannot stand it."

"Bring him back, Lord, bring him back," prays a young fellow of nineteen near the door. "Don't let Thy judgement fall upon him. He has felt the Spirit moving - he said so - but he is fleeing. Bring him back." "He will come back, friend," the missioner assures us, "he will come back; the fact that he has run away is a proof that he will come back."

The next question is one that gives relief ---

(4) "All those who want to love the Lord Jesus, will they stand up?"

There is now not a single seat occupied. Members, nonmembers, sceptics, scoffers - all, all are on their feet, and the silence that supervenes is oppressive. But the missioner is all happiness and smiles.

Presently we are singing that inspiring hymn of praise -

> Duw mawr y rhyfeddodau maith
> Rhyfeddol yw pob rhan o'th waith.

And we are reminded by the missioner that in that hymn we are addressing God Himself and that if we cannot sing with all our hearts we had better be silent.

In the same issue the reporter publishes a special message given him by Mr. Roberts for the public. After emphatically disclaiming any share in the religious upheaval, which he attributed solely to the Holy Spirit, Mr. Roberts said:

"I will give you a message. I should like the people to believe. They wait for me. They should wait only for the Spirit. Someone said they are almost breaking their heart for me to go. Will they almost break their heart for the Holy Spirit? Then It must come down. What does the Word say? Ask and receive. It is just that. Ask and ye shall receive. That is the promise. Believe it. Don't wait for me. Some are talking of the share that this denomination or that has in the work. It is not denominational. In Loughor we had all denominations - Methodists, Churchmen, Congregationalists, Baptists, every one."

"Give me a message distinct, plain, for the people, Mr. Roberts."

He waited a minute or two before answering, and then said:

"This is the message. Of course I had to pray for it. To ask for guidance how the prophecy of Joel is being fulfilled. There the Lord says, 'I will pour out my Spirit upon all flesh.' If that be so all flesh must be prepared to receive it. Note the four conditions:

"First. The past must be clear: every sin confessed to God. Any wrong put upon any man must be made right.

"Second. Everything doubtful must be removed once and for all out of our lives.

"Third. Obedience prompt and implicit to the Holy Spirit.

"Fourth. Public confession must be made of Christ.

"These are the four conditions given. If every Church wilt comply with these four conditions, then all will be made one. Once the Spirit comes down and takes possession of a man, he is made one with Christ and one with all men. All denominations are one. You know what Christ said, 'I, if I be lifted up, will draw all men unto Me.' There it is, Christ is all in all."

Mr. Roberts indulges in no invectives against anything or anybody. He does not even denounce the publican. At one meeting, on December 4th, he heard a young fellow declaring, "A week ago I was blind drunk; today I am free, and the craving is gone." "Aye, aye," exclaims the missioner, "and there's no need to preach against the drink; but preach Christ, proclaim Christ unto the people: that is all sufficient."

The truth about Evan Roberts is that he is very psychic, with clairvoyance well developed and a strong visualizing gift. One peculiarity about him is that he has not yet found any watch that will keep time when it is carried in his pocket. Many of his visions are merely the vivid visualization of mental concepts, as, for instance, when he says:

> "When I go out to the garden I see the devil grinning at me, but I am not afraid of him; I go into the house, and when I go out again to the back I see Jesus Christ smiling at me. Then I know all is well."

This, again, is much the same thing:

> While listening to a sermon at Newcastle Emlyn once, he said, he received much more of the Spirit of the Gospel from what he saw than from what he heard. The preacher was doing very well, was warming with his work, and sweating by the very energy of his delivery. And when he (Evan Roberts) saw the sweat on the preachers brow he looked beyond and

saw another vision: his Lord sweating the bloody sweat in the garden (and then, as Mr. Roberts thought of the vision, he utterly broke down).

The missioners go like the Friars of old, or like the Seventy in the Gospel, without money and without scrip. As Sir A. Thomas said, the Revival finances itself. There are no bills, no halls, no salaries.

Chapter 5
The Rise and Progress of The Revival

Mr. George Meredith once remarked that one great secret of the triumph of Christianity over the paganism of imperial Rome was the astonishing discovery made by the Apostle Paul as to the value of women as religious teachers. Before his time women served in the sanctuary indeed, but as creatures of sense, for the degradation rather than as embodiments of souls capable of inspiring and uplifting the human race. Paul, it is true, when introducing so great an innovation, found it necessary, while addressing the Church of Corinth, to draw a very hard and fast line limiting the sphere of female activity; and this limitation, which was local and temporary, being necessitated solely by the corruption of sex morality in Corinth at that time, has been used, no doubt to the Apostles infinite chagrin, to limit the beneficent action of women in the ministry of the Church in other ages and in other climes. Christianity, however, is at last sloughing the Corinthian limitation and asserting the full freedom which Paul secured for women elsewhere. The Quakers began the good work. The Methodists did something in the same direction. It was reserved for the Salvation Army, the only religious organization founded by a husband and wife acting in absolute unity, to make the equality of the sexes a chief comer-stone. Now in South Wales we see the fruits of this devoted testimony. The Welsh, down to the time of the last Revival, were in the bonds of the Corinthian limitation. Even in the sixties a lady lecturer on temperance was looked at askance in many parts of Wales.

Now all that has gone by the board. In the present Revival

women are everywhere to the fore, singing, testifying, praying, and preaching. Dr. Henry Rees, who protested publicly in 1866 against the ministry of women, appears to be dead, and his spirit has died with him. At last these good people have realized the great saying that in Christ there is neither bond nor free, so there is neither male nor female. The change is so marked that it suggests the happy thought that as the Revival of 1859 to 1861 led to the enfranchisement of the male householder, the present Revival may be crowned by the recognition by the State of the full citizenship of women.

Women came into this Revival chiefly as singers, but they soon found that the ministry of sacred song needed to be supplemented by that of prayer and of exhortation. But even if they had done nothing but sing, they would have had a leading part in this Revival. For it is as Dr. Joseph Parry predicted, as long ago as 1891, that it would be a singing Revival.

How did it begin, this Revival? Where was it nursed into being? What influences nurtured it into the full maturity of its powers?

For a long time past the Welsh Christians had been moved to pray specially for the quickening of religious life in their midst. The impulse appears to have been sporadic and spontaneous. In remote country hamlets, in mining villages buried in distant valleys, one man or one woman would have it laid upon his or her soul to pray that the Holy Spirit might be poured out upon the cause in which they were spiritually concerned. There does not seem to have been much organized effort. It was all individual, local, and strictly limited to the neighborhood.

But prayer circles formed by devout persons who agree to unite together in prayer at a given hour every day have long been a recognized form of prevailing prayer. By these circles there are some thirty or forty thousand people now banded together to pray for a world-wide Revival.

All this was general. It was preparing the way. A great longing for Revival was abroad in the land. The Churches were conscious that there was something in the air. It was at New Quay, in Cardiganshire, that the spark appears to have first fired the charged train

of religious emotion. Fortunately, we have from the Rev. Joseph
Jenkins, the pastor of the Calvinistic Church in which the Revival
first made its appearance, an authentic account of its beginning.
The first person to be awakened was the pastor himself. He was a
good man, a devoted Christian, and a faithful minister; but, like
Evan Roberts, he felt that there was still something lacking. It was
before Midsummer, 1903, that the conviction was borne in upon
the good pastor's mind that the occasion had come for special services with greater freedom for testifying. It was his own quickened
spiritual experience which sought the institution of these meetings
as a means of giving expression to the life of the Church.

The meetings he had in view were to have no set form. They
must be free, each to assume its own peculiar form spontaneously.
Those present would be expected to pray, sing, read, or speak, according to the impulse of the moment. He longed to pour his spiritual experience into sympathetic ears. He found himself frequently
in close communion with his heavenly Father, and seemed to be
given everything necessary to efficient service. He related his experience in fear and trembling. He felt that he himself must have been
saved many years ago, although he had missed the joy which the
knowledge of such a fact brings. He had no doubt that his efforts to
preach Christ had been honest, and that he had done his best to obtain for himself also some of the benefits of his preaching. And yet
he had never before understood the Gospel as he understands it today - the power of God unto present assurance of full salvation.

Some time ago --- the preacher was speaking in November, and
his sermon was reported in *The South Wales Daily News* of November 16th, and no more precise date is given --- the experience
occurred which may be regarded as the first outward and visible
sign of the Revival. I give the story as it is reported. A "Seiat" appears to be a religious meeting for prayer:

> Some time ago he had returned from a journey, and found
> that a Seiat had been set aside in favor of a soirée to be held
> in the town. Somebody rose at one of the church meetings
> and asked why the Seiat was being set aside - the soirée was

not a sufficient reason. It was decided to hold a Seiat, and in that meeting were seen and heard the first indications of the day-spring from on high that was surely dawning upon the church. A young girl prayed, and that prayer was the most wonderful and touching he had ever heard,, The response was immediate. All were lifted up into a high plane of spiritual experience. One of the older deacons, who was standing by the door, came forward. Hot tears were rolling down his face when he said, "It's all right, I know Him. He is the Holy Spirit."

The minister as he sat marveled at the signs of the new experience that he knew must be coming to the church. Nevertheless, his heart was not perfectly right before the Lord. A brother minister with whom he had spent a night had, in course of conversation upon religious matters, said to him very straightforwardly, "My friend, I am afraid you are backsliding, there is something in your view of things, and in the cadences of your voice, that betokens serious backsliding in your spiritual life." It was too true, he admitted - and the charge went home. The conviction of its truth and of its guilt sank deep into his soul. A bosom friend -- Mr. Ceredig Evans -- to whom he told his experience, wept and prayed with him, and promised to continue at the Throne of Grace on his behalf. He was perfectly convinced that the matter of his soul as between himself and God was not settled altogether in God's way. A Voice Within him demanded work of him, demanded the fulfilment of his ministry. He was shown others with humbler talents, as he was told, yet with far better records of real work done in the Master's vineyard. His wife was present, and knew all his private experience in this matter - how he prayed all night, and night after night he continued to pray and read, until one night in his study, in the small hours of the morning, a vision of the Cross arose filling his soul with joy and peace.

Here again we have the vision. "In point of fact," says Professor James, "you will hardly find a religious leader of any kind in whose life there is no record of such things. St. Paul had his visions, his ecstasies, his gift of tongues. The whole array of Christian saints and heresiarchs, including the greatest, the Bernards, the Loyolas, the Luthers, the Foxes, the Wesleys, had these visions, voices, rapt conditions, guiding impressions, and openings. They had these things because they had exalted sensibility, and to such things persons of exalted sensibility are liable."

Pastor Jenkins, having thus entered into a new and fuller relation with the Spirit, summoned his young people to the new kind of meetings which he saw were called for. They were well attended, and were conducted on the principle of leaving everyone free to pray, sing, and speak, or sit silent as the Spirit moved them.

One Sunday night he preached from the text, "This is the victory that overcometh the world, even our faith." He had preached before on some phases of that subject, but now he felt his very soul go out in his words, which God blessed immediately. That night a young girl came to his house to consult him concerning the salvation of her soul. She did not know how she should speak to him, and remained walking to and fro outside the house for some time. But she was intensely in earnest, and, courage coming, she entered the house. He advised her to receive Jesus as her Savior, but that she must receive Him as Lord as well as Savior - she must surrender all to Him. She must pray until her soul allowed the matter to be settled on God's terms. She promised to follow his advice, and she did, for her soul was moved to its lowest depth. A Christian Endeavour meeting was coming, and he would then see how far they under-stood spiritual experience. He spoke, explaining it in the best way he could, and with all the force at his command. Others followed with speeches, but he required of them expressions of spiritual experience pure and simple, and then it was that the young girl already referred to stood up, and with beaming face and thrilling voice said, "Oh, I love Jesus with all my heart." After this, spiritual history was made rapidly at the Christian Endeavour meetings, some revealing great depths of emotion, others manifesting the keenest sense of spiritual relations.

That public confession of her faith by the young girl - who may be regarded as the first convert of the Revival - was followed by others. It was evident the Revival had come. One Christian Endeavored, who had prepared a paper to read on the existence of God, could not bring himself to read it for the same reason that Professor James dismisses the arguments of philosophy as a foundation for religion. It said that spiritually the meeting was far in advance of his paper. The Christian Endeavorers had the proofs of His existence in their own hearts. There was no shadow of doubt of His existence. He was there amongst them then, transforming their very lives. In this way their meetings were started. From New Quay, which lies midway between Cardigan and Aberystwyth, the Christian Endeavorers went out to hold meetings elsewhere. Among other places, they went to Newcastle Emlyn, where they met Evan Roberts.

So far as I can fix it from the materials at my disposal, the public confession of the young girl which marks the beginning of the Revival occurred in New Quay on February, 1904.

It was in September that Evan Roberts prayed at the New Quay Christian Endeavorers' meeting and saw the visions which directed him to Loughor. It was in the beginning of November he began to hold the special services at Loughor, which attracted the attention of the press. After that the full reports of the proceedings in *The Western Mail* and *The Cardiff Daily News* spread the revival through the whole of South Wales.

It is worthy of note that the great Revival of 1859 also began in Cardiganshire, although somewhat farther to the north than New Quay. The following notes as to the places visited by Mr. Evan Roberts will give those who know the district, but to no one else, some idea how the fire spread along the valleys of Wales.

November 14th and 15th, Trecynon; November 16th to 18th, Pontycymmer; November 19th, Bridgend, Pyle, Abergwyn, November 20th, Abercynon; November 21st and 22nd, Mountain Ash; November 23rd and 24th, Ynysybwl; November 25th, ill; November 26th, Cilfyngdd; November 27th and 28th, Porth; November 29th, Treorky; December 2nd to 4th, Pentre; December 5th and 6th, Caerphilly; December 7th, Senghenydd; December 8th to 10th, Ferndale; December 11th, Marely; December 12th and 13th, Tylorstown; December 14th and 15th, Aberfan; December 16th and 17th, Hafod (Pontypriddl; December 18th,Pontypridd; December 19th and 20th, Clydach Vale; December 21st, Tonypandy; December 22nd, Penygraig; December 23rd, Treherbert.

"The supreme test of a Revival," says the Rev. F. B. Meyer," is the ethical result." As to this the testimony of all on the spot is unanimous. Not merely are all the grosser vices reduced to vanishing point, but the subtler sins of unforgiving rancour, non-payment of debts, dishonest work are abated. In nothing is Mr. Evan Roberts clearer and more emphatic than in his insistence upon forgiveness of injuries, unless it be as to the duty of the payment of debts. "It's no use asking God to forgive you," he tells his hearers, "unless you have forgiven all your enemies -- everyone. You will only be forgiven in the same measure as you forgive." Again he says: "How can there be, when there are family feuds and personal animosities, churches torn by little dissensions, members cold towards each other? If you are not prepared to forgive others it is no use going on your knees tonight to ask God to forgive your transgressions. I don't say don't do it, please yourselves, of course; but one thing is absolutely certain, God will not listen to you."

The result has been excellent - everywhere excellent.

However we may explain it, the worst sceptic must admit that what the Revivalist seeks to effect is of all things the most important object of human endeavor. No political or social change can be regarded as having any serious importance, excepting so far as it tends to facilitate indirectly the achievement of the same result which the Revivalist seeks directly. The aim of all reformers is the regeneration of the individual. To make a bad man good, a cruel man merciful, a lazy man industrious, a drunkard sober, and to substitute selfless struggle to help others for a selfish scramble to seize everything for oneself - that in the aim-all, the be-all, and the end-all of all those who seek the improvement of society and the progress of the world. It makes no difference whether the reformer is called Blatchford or Liddon, Bradlaugh or Price Hughes, John Morley or General Booth, Frederic Harrison or the Archbishop of Canterbury, the President of the Free Thinkers' Congress or the Pope of Rome - that is what they are all after - that, and in the ultimate, nothing but that. And when it comes to be looked at scientifically, who can deny that a great religious Revival often succeeds in achieving the result which we all desire more rapidly, more decisively, and in a greater number of cases, than any other agency known to mankind? We may discount it as much as we like. But the facts are there. It is not necessary to credit the Revival with all the results which it reveals, any more than we may credit a day's sunshine in spring with all the flowers it brings to birth. But it brings them out. So does a Revival. And if there had been no Revival, the latent sainthood of multitudes would never have been born, just as the flowers would never come out in May if there were no sun.

It is often argued that Revivalism is ephemeral. But as our brief historical retrospect shows, the fruit of Revivals are among the most permanent things in history.

Chapter 6
What Ought I To Do?

SPREAD the good news, and spread it now!

If you can do nothing else, send copies of this pamphlet to any relative, friend, or other person whom you think may become interested in the subject. Speak to people about it. Write to your friends about it.

If you belong to a Church, try to get the members interested in the Revival.

If you are a minister, preach about it, and ask your people to hold prayer meetings on the subject.

For if those who have seen most of the Revival are right, there is a great blessing in this movement for each of us, and for all of us, if we but make the most of our present opportunity.

What we have to do is to take time by the forelock and be ready to clutch the boon before the moment has passed. As a start, we might well begin each in our sphere by doing good turns to our enemies, wiping out the memories of old grudges, reconciling offended relatives, and forgiving others, even as we hope to be forgiven.

God or no God, soul or no soul, this earth is made much more like Hell than Heaven by persisting in these grudges, jealousies, animosities, and unkind feelings one towards another. What a merry Christmas, what a glad New Year it would be if we could begin by being in charity with everybody, in love with every man, woman, and child with whom we have a personal acquaintance!

Then when we have cast out from our own souls the evil spirits of Bitterness, Rancor, Unfriendliness, jealousy, and have forgiven all those who have injured us, or, a much harder task, whom we have injured, we shall be better prepared to receive the outpouring of the Divine blessing which we all profess to desire.

After the Revival has come, as come it will if we but make room for it by ejecting hatred, malice, and uncharitableness from our hearts, then a great duty will be laid upon the Churches to supply fresh interests for the new converts, who have given up everything that filled their leisure. The Rev. Dr. Morris, of Treorky, an ex-president of the Baptist Union, told an interviewer of *The South Wales Daily News* that he at least is fully alive to the importance of this subject:

"Do you know," he said, "this Revival has thrown a tremendous responsibility upon the Churches? Public-houses and football fields are being emptied of young men. What are the Churches going to do with them? Unfortunately, we in Wales are lamentably deficient in provision for the development of the body, mind, and spirit of a man. I agree absolutely with the leading articles in *The South Wales Daily News*, when they urge that Christianity should provide for the education and development of the whole of a man, and not merely a part of him. The Churches have been brought face to face with a difficult problem. How shall we keep our young people, now that they have been induced to join the Church? In small places there is no attraction in the Church; no accommodation is attempted for their moral well-being."

"What would you suggest as a means of meeting this contingency?"

"My suggestion would be the provision of an Institutional Church. There should be young men's and young women's parlors, separate classrooms, lecture rooms, museums, and libraries. I would also advise the encouragement of physical culture -- of course, we must guard against extremes -- but some means must be devised to hold our young people, otherwise a great part of the good effect of the Revival will be lost."

Upon this question possibly some hints may be gained from my Christmas story, "Here Am I: Send Me!"

Part 2
Chapter 7: The Revival: Its Power and Source
By Rev. G. Campbell Morgan, D. D., London

[We are permitted by Dr. Morgan, who controls the copyright, to condense into the following article a recent sermon by him to his people at Westminster Chapel, London, and published in the Christian Commonwealth.—Editor.]

It was my holy privilege to come into the center of this wonderful work and movement. Arriving in the morning in the village, everything seemed quiet, and we wended our way to the place where a group of chapels stood. Oh, these chapels through Wales! Thank God for them! Everything was so quiet and orderly that we had to ask where the meeting was. A lad, pointing to a chapel, said, "In there." Not a single person outside. We made our way through the open door, and just managed to get inside, and found the chapel crowded from floor to ceiling with a great mass of people.

The Three Characteristics Of The Meetings

It was a meeting characterized by a perpetual series of interruptions and disorderliness. It was a meeting characterized by a great continuity and an absolute order. You say, "How do you reconcile these things?" I do not reconcile them. They are both there. If you put a man into the midst of one of these meetings who knows nothing of the language of the Spirit, and nothing of the life of the Spirit, one of two things will happen to him. He will either pass out saying, "These men are drunk," or he himself will be swept up by the fire into the kingdom of God. If you put a man down who knows the language of the Spirit, he will be struck by this most peculiar thing. I have never seen anything like it in my life; while a man praying is disturbed by the breaking out of song, there is no sense of disorder, and the prayer merges into song, and back into testimony, and back again into song for hour after hour, without guidance. These are the three occupations— singing, prayer, testimony.

In the afternoon we were at another chapel, and another meeting, equally full, and this time Evan Roberts was present. He came into the meeting when it had been on for an hour and a half. He spoke, but his address—if it could be called an address—was punctuated perpetually by song and prayer and testimony. Evan Roberts works on that plan, never hindering any one. I venture to say that if that address Evan Roberts gave in broken fragments had been reported, the whole of it could have been read in six or seven minutes. As the meeting went on, a man rose in the gallery and said, "So and So," naming some man, "has decided for Christ," and then in a moment the song began. They did not sing Songs of Praises, they sang Diolch Iddo, and the weirdness and beauty of it swept over the audience. It was a song of praise because that man was born again. There are no inquiry rooms, no penitent forms, but some worker announces, or an inquirer openly confesses Christ, the name is registered and the song breaks out, and they go back to testimony and prayer.

In the evening I stood for three solid hours wedged so that I could not lift my hands at all. That which impressed me most was the congregation. I stood wedged, and I looked along the gallery of the chapel on my right, and there were three women, and the rest were men packed solidly in. If you could but for once have seen the men, evidently colliers, with the blue seam that told of their work on their faces, clean and beautiful. Beautiful, did I say? Many of them lit with heaven's own light, radiant with the light that never was on sea and land. Great rough, magnificent, poetic men by nature, but the nature had slumbered long. To-day it is awakened, and

I looked on many a face, and I knew that men did not see me, did not see Evan Roberts, but they saw the face of God and the eternities. I left that evening, after having been in the meeting three hours, at 10:30, and it swept on, packed as it was, until an early hour next morning, song and prayer and testimony and conversion and confession of sin by leading church-members publicly, and the putting of it away, and all the while no human leader, no one indicating the next thing to do, no one checking the spontaneous movement.

The Man Himself

Evan Roberts is hardly more than a boy, simple and natural, no orator; with nothing of the masterfulness that characterized such men as Wesley and Whitefield and Dwight Lyman Moody; no leader of men. One of the most brilliant writers in one of our papers said of Evan Roberts, in a tone of sorrow, that he lacked the qualities of leadership, and the writer said if but some prophet did now arise he could sweep everything before him. God has not chosen that a prophet shall arise. It is quite true. Evan Roberts is no orator, no leader. What is he? I mean now with regard to this great movement. He is the mouthpiece of the fact that there is no human guidance as to man or organization. The burden of what he says to the people is this: It is not man; do not wait for me; depend on God; obey the Spirit. But whenever moved to do so, he speaks under the guidance of the Spirit. His work is not that of appealing to men so much as that of creating an atmosphere by calling men to follow the guidance of the Spirit in whatever the Spirit shall say to them.

God has set his hand upon the lad, beautiful in simplicity, ordained in his devotion, lacking all the qualities that we have looked for in preachers and prophets and leaders. He has put him in the forefront of this movement that the world may see that he does choose the things that are not to bring to naught the things that are, the weak things of the world to confound the things that are mighty; a man who lacks all the essential qualities which we say make for greatness, in order that through him in simplicity and power he may move to victory.

Peculiarities Of The Movement

There is no preaching, no order, no hymn books, no choirs, no organs, no collections and, finally, no advertising. I am not saying these things are wrong. I simply want you to see what God is doing. There were the organs, but silent; the ministers, but among the rest of the people, rejoicing and prophesying with the rest, only there was no preaching. Everybody is preaching. No order, and yet it moves from day to day, week to week, county to county, with matchless precision, with the order of an attacking force. Mr. Stead was asked if he thought the revival would spread to London, and he said, "It depends upon whether you can sing." He was not so wide of the mark. When these Welshmen sing, they sing the words like men who believe them. They abandon themselves to their singing. We sing as though we thought it would not be respectable to be heard by the man next to us. No choir, did I say? It was all choir. And hymns! I stood and listened in wonder and amazement as that congregation on that night sang hymn after hymn, long hymns, sung through without hymn-books.

The Sunday-school is having its harvest now. The family altar is having its harvest now. The teaching of hymns and the Bible among those Welsh hills and valleys is having its harvest now. No advertising. The whole thing advertises itself. You tell me the press is advertising it. They did not begin advertising until the thing caught fire and spread. One of the most remarkable things is the attitude of the Welsh press. I come across instance after instance of men converted by reading the story of the revival in *The Western Mail* and *The South Wales Daily News*.

The Origin Of The Movement

In the name of God let us all cease trying to find it. At least let us cease trying to trace it to any one man or convention. You cannot trace it, and yet I will trace it tonight. Whence has it come? All over Wales—I am giving you roughly the result of the questioning of fifty or more persons at random in the week—a praying remnant have been agonizing before God about the state of the beloved land, and it is through that the answer of fire has come. You tell me that the revival originates with Roberts. I tell you that Roberts is a product of the revival. You tell me that it began in an Endeavor meeting where a dear girl bore testimony. I tell you that was part of the result of a revival breaking out everywhere. If you and I could stand above Wales, looking at it, you would see fire breaking out here and there, and yonder, and somewhere else, without any collusion or prearrangement. It is a divine visitation in which God—let me say this reverently—in which God is saying to us: See what I can do without the things you are depending on; see what I can do in answer to a praying people; see what I can do through the simplest who are ready to fall in line and depend wholly and absolutely upon me.

A Church Revival

What is the character of this revival? It is a church revival. I do not mean by that merely a revival among church members. It is that, but it is held in church buildings. I have been saying for a long time that the revival which is to be permanent in the life of a nation must be associated with the life of the churches. What I am looking for is that there shall come a revival breaking out in all our regular church life. The meetings are held in the chapels, all up and down the valleys, and it began among church members, and when it touches the outside man it makes him into a church-member at once. I am tremendously suspicious of any mission or revival movement that treats with contempt the Church of Christ, and affects to despise the churches. Within five weeks twenty thousand have joined the churches. I think more than that have been converted, but the churches in Wales have enrolled during the last five weeks twenty thousand new members. It is a movement in the Church and of the Church, a movement in which the true functions and forces of the Church are being exercised and filled.

Striking Cases Of Personal Influence

What effect is this work producing upon men? First of all, it is turning Christians everywhere into evangelists. There is nothing more remarkable about it than that, I think. People you never expected to see doing this kind of thing are becoming definite personal workers. A friend of mine went to one of the meetings, and he walked down to the meeting with an old friend of his, a deacon of the Congregational church, a man whose piety no one doubted, a man who for long years had worked in the life of the church in some of its departments, but a man who never would think of speaking to men about their souls, although he would not have objected to someone else doing it. As my friend walked down with the deacon, the deacon said to him: "I have eighteen young men in an athletic class of which I am president. I hope some of them will be in the meeting tonight." There was a new manifestation. This man had had that athletic class for years, and he had never hoped that any one of them would be in any meeting to be saved. Within fifteen minutes he left his seat by my friend and was seen talking to a young man down in front of him. Presently this deacon rose and said, "Thank God for So and So," giving his name; "he has given his heart to Christ right here." In a moment or two he left him, and was with another young man. Before that meeting closed that deacon had led every one of those eighteen young men to Jesus Christ, who never before thought of speaking to men about their souls.

My own friend, with whom I stayed, who has always been reticent of speaking to men, told me how, sitting in his office, there surged upon him the great conviction that he ought to go and speak to another man with whom he had done business for long years. My friend suddenly put down his pen and left his office and went on 'Change, and there he saw the very man; and going up to him, passing the time of day to him, the man said to him, "What do you think of this revival?" And my friend looked him squarely in the eye and said, "How is it with your own soul?" The man looked back at him and said, "Last night at twelve, for some unknown reason, I had to get out of bed and give myself to Jesus Christ, and I was hungering for some one to come and talk to me." Here is a man turned into an evangelist by supernatural means. If this is emotional, then God send us more of it! Here is a cool, calculating, business ship owner, that I have known all my life, leaving his office to go on 'Change and ask a man about his soul.

Down in one of the mines a collier was walking along, and he came, to his great surprise, to where one of the principal officials in the mine was standing. The official said, "Jim, I have been waiting two hours here for you." "Have you, sir?" said Jim. "What do you want?" "I want to be saved, Jim." The man said, "Let us get right down here"; and there in the mine the colliery official, instructed by the collier, passed into the kingdom of God. When he got up he said, "Tell all the men, tell everybody you meet, I am converted."

The movement is characterized by the most remarkable confession of sin—confessions that must be costly. I heard some of them, men rising who have been members of the church and officers of the church, confessing hidden sin in their heart, impurity committed and condoned, and seeking prayer for its putting away. The whole movement is marvelously characterized by a confession of Jesus Christ, testimony to his power, to his goodness, to his beneficence, and testimony merging forevermore into outbursts of singing.

This whole thing is of God; it is a visitation in which he is making men conscious of Himself, without any human agency. The revival is far more wide-spread than the fire zone. In this sense you may understand that the fire zone is where the meetings are actually held, and where you feel the flame that burns. But even when you come out of it, and go into railway trains, or into a shop, a bank, anywhere, men everywhere are talking of God. Whether they obey or not is another matter. There are thousands not yielded to the constraint of God, but God has given Wales in these days a new conviction and consciousness of himself. That is the profound thing, the underlying truth.

BOOK TWO

The Story of the Welsh Revival:

As Told By Eyewitnesses . . .

The Story of the Welsh Revival

1: A Message to the World
By Evan Roberts

THE Power of the revival in South Wales is not of men, but of God. He has been close to us and has shown us the way.

There is no question of creed or of dogma in this movement. The work that is being done has the support, I believe, of all Christian people and Christian churches in our country. I have merely preached the religion of Jesus Christ as I myself have experienced it.

God has "made me glad," and I am showing others the great joy of serving Him, a joy so great and so wonderful that I shall never be able to express it in its completeness. We are teaching no sectarian doctrine, only the wonder and the beauty of Christ's love, the love of man for Him, and the love of man for man.

I have been asked concerning my methods. I have none. I never prepare the words I shall speak. I leave all that to Him. I am not the source of this revival. I am only one agent in what is growing to be a multitude. I am not moving men's hearts and changing men's lives; not I, but "God worketh in me." I have found what is, in my belief, the highest kind of Christianity. I desire to give my life, which is all I have to give, to helping others to find it also. Many have already found it, thank God, and many more are finding it through them.

This is my work as He has pointed it out to me. His Spirit came to me one night, when upon my knees I asked Him for guidance, and five months later I was baptized with the Spirit. He has led me as He will lead all those who, conscious of their human weakness, lean upon Him as children upon a father. I know that the work which has been done through me is not due to any human ability that I possess. It is His work and to His Glory. "I was not ever thus, nor prayed that Thou should'st lead me on. I loved to choose and see my path, but now lead Thou me on."

I desire nothing but to be allowed to continue this work that has begun. "The Lord is my Shepherd. I fear no want." All things necessary He has provided, and will provide. I wish no personal following, only the world for Christ.

Some things have been said about our meetings, and about me which are not true; but God's truth has not been hurt by these misstatements, and they, therefore, matter little. I believe, too, that He has put it into the hearts of those who have written of the revival to say helpful things, for some of the papers have carried our message to many whom we have not personally reached.

I believe that the world is upon the threshold of a great religious revival, and I pray daily that I may be allowed to help bring this about. I beseech all those who confess Christ to ask Him today, upon their knees, if He has not some work for them to do now. He will lead them all as He has led us. He will make them pillars of smoke by day and pillars of fire by night to guide all men to Him.

I beseech all those who confess Christ to ask Him today, upon their knees, if He has not some work for them to do now. He will lead them all as He has led us. He will make them pillars of smoke by day and pillars of fire by night to guide all men to Him.

Wonderful things have happened in Wales in a few weeks, but these are only a beginning. The world will be swept by His Spirit as by a rushing, mighty wind. Many who are now silent Christians, negative Christians, Christians whose belief means little to them and nothing to anyone else, will lead in the movement. Groping, hesitating, half-hearted Christians will see a great Light and will reflect this Light to thousands of those in utter darkness. The whole world will hear His message of "peace, good-will toward men," and listening, will be blessed. Thousands upon thousands will do more than we have accomplished, as God gives them power. This is my earnest faith, if the churches will but learn the great lesson of obedience to the voice of the Holy Spirit. Obedience! Obedience!! Obedience!!!

2: The Story of the Welsh Revival
By Arthur Goodrich

All South Wales is aflame with the spirit of a great religious revival. In a few weeks the fire of it has run up and down the length of the Garw Valley and the Rhondda, and has spread into hundreds of little outlying hamlets, where in steady, deadening routine the men work in the black coalpit through all the glorious days that come in that wonderful country of mountains and sunshine and clear air.

They are talking of little else in the snug little stone cottages that line the ridges like low ramparts; in the tiny shops where the women come to buy the day's supplies; in the railway carriages, and at the street corners. Every church community is stirred to the depths, and out on the edges rough miners are shaking their heads wonderingly, and are being drawn toward it until the power of it seizes them and they leave their work to attend the day meetings as well as those at night. Strong men are in tears of penitence; women are shaken with a new fervor, and in the streets small children at their play are humming revival hymns.

"And they do say that the publicans (saloon keepers) are closing," says a bent little man with a black beard, in a train to Landore, and certainly many drinking places that were crowded are empty, the frequenters being led away either by the religious workers in person, as they were at Ponticymmer, or by the irresistible spirit of the movement.

"Aye," says another, "there's something funny about it. They say you feel it as soon as you're inside the building where he's going to speak."

"He," is Evan Roberts, the young Lougher lad of 26 years, who alone among men has "fired up" the mining valleys, and who dominates the entire revival with a power which, as he says earnestly, is not from within him, but from above; the Spirit which led him to do what he has done.

In a railway carriage, men who have not seen him repeat with awe the stories they read in the papers, how he is pale-faced, and how he says his body is electrified, and how he has visions, and what a strange light he has in his eyes, and how he get's only an hour's sleep in a night, and has no watch that will keep time in his pocket, most of which is, of course, mere talk, and if true at all, true only in part.

Others, coming from their first meeting, are obviously perplexed at the man's grip upon people, and yet they themselves have felt it, and hurry away to think by themselves whether the way he has pointed for them is not best after all.

And strangers— standing before a wayside chapel in the midst of farming land and seeing the men and women come hurrying from up and down the narrow road, or sitting in some larger building where the aisles are packed to the doors with miners and miners' sons and wives and daughters, and beyond, into the hallway, and perhaps into the street outside— ask, as they look about at hard faces softening under the simple spell of the missioner's talk, who this young man is who can work such wonders in a few weeks, and where he came from, and how it has all come about.

For an answer to this we must go back to Lougher, a little mining town near Swansea, and back, also, a number of years, and the story of Evan Roberts, the man, explains much of the secret of his power.

Fifteen minutes' walk from Lougher station, in a district known as Gorseinon, is the little house of a hard-working, God-fearing miner. It is on a side road, and from where it stands you can look off across swampland to a great black colliery on the left, and beyond to the long range of the hills of Llanganech. The house is of stone, plastered over with cement and lime, hardened to a light brown, corduroy appearance. A gate leads to an inner path, and another gate to the front door, hidden from the road by profuse hedges and greenery.

At the back is a large garden which has to do with the story, and within, in the quaint, scrupulously clean general room, is the melodeon, beside which Evan Roberts and his brother Dan, who is helping him now in his work, sang the stirring Welsh hymns from their boyhood. And no one who has met the kindly, quiet, lovable personality of Evan Roberts' mother, or who has seen the light of her great faith in her eyes, will fail to realise how much he, and how much South Wales, and perhaps the world, owes to her.

Evan Roberts is one of her seven sons, of whom only three are now living; and in all Lougher not a word can be said against him, and no man remembers anything but good of him.

As one man, who was evidently not greatly moved by the spirit of the revival, said to me: "Whatever else can be said about Evan Roberts, he was always good, always honest, straightforward and earnest." Indeed, the feeling of Lougher for him is summed up in the words of a good woman who showed me the way to his home. "Evan Roberts, God bless him," she said; and South Wales is catching phrase.

Women whose husbands had sunk into sordid degradation, and whom he has brought back to them out of the pit, are saying it; mothers whose sons have exchanged the public-house for the chapel, are repeating it; friends of men like Tom Hughes, the atheist, of Aberdare, who has burned his books of unbelief and is working and praying day and night for those who, like him, belonged to the so-called Ethical Society, are saying it; and the hundreds of men and women who have found a new guide for their hesitating steps, are crying it, singing it, praying it.

It is one of those simple homes— and there are many like it in South Wales— about which one feels unconsciously that every stone was laid with a prayer, and every board with a hymn.

The atmosphere of it is of steady, honest toil, of frugal living, and of an unquestioning, vital religious faith. And it was in this kind of a home that Evan Roberts lived during his boyhood. It had its share of trouble; times were not always good; the family was large, and a coal miner seldom receives more money than just enough to keep his home and to do his share toward the support of the chapel; but there was always in this home that beautiful, whole-souled trust in God which crowded out any gloom from their lives.

When he was about twelve his father had a serious accident. He fell and hurt his foot so badly that he was told it would be four months before be could go back to his work in the mines, for Mr. Roberts' work kept him constantly on his feet.

He was needed at the colliery, and, when they learned how long it would be before he could do all that they depended upon him to do, they came and asked him if he couldn't come with one of his boys, keeping quiet himself and getting the boy to run here and there for him. And this was the way in which Evan Roberts first went into the Mountain Colliery— to help his father until Mr. Roberts was well. A few shillings every week, also, the father gave the boy for his help— the first money Evan Roberts earned.

When Mr. Roberts was able to do all of his work again, the boy was given a task of opening and shutting the doors for the cars in the mine, and after a time he became a "knocker."

When he was just old enough to understand something of what a religious life meant, he heard one of the church deacons say at one of the week-day meetings— and he always attended these as well as the Sunday services— that if they prayed and waited in a prayerful spirit, sometime the Holy Spirit would come to them.

From that night this became the great desire of Evan Roberts' life, and be lived on gropingly, hoping, praying, believing that someday he would come into a full realization of what was to him the one important thing in life complete communion with God. He had from the beginning the fundamental, implicit faith of the woman who touched the hem of His garment.

At night when he came home from the colliery, unless there was a meeting at the church, he settled down to his books, and he spent his carefully saved money for more books.

Among other things he learned shorthand, and he has what I have never seen before— a shorthand Bible. And, indeed, in whatever he did the Bible was always his greatest book— the one that he read constantly and with increasing insight.

As he grew older he began to take part in the meetings, and one evening, when he was away from home, he talked at a service in another town nearby. And what he said was so clear and forcible, and he said it in so vigorous and earnest a fashion, that the minister came to him after the meeting and told him that he ought to become a preacher.

Nobody at Lougher, even in his home, heard of this until someone else repeated it to them. For Evan Roberts is very silent about himself. his thought, I believe, has always been much more for the faith than for any part he himself might play in spreading it to others.

For years his life was a steady, simple routine. In the mornings he went to the mines, either at the Gorseinon Colliery or at Mountain Ash, where he worked for a time. All day long there was the hard toil that stiffened the fiber of his body, and the dealing with hard, older men, that strengthened the fiber of his soul. And at night he studied and read, and sang, and prayed, even as he worked, honestly and earnestly.

Evan Roberts, in whatever he has done from childhood, has "meant intensely and meant good." And wherever he went people of all ages liked him for his manly vigor and for his unceasing cheeriness.

He was a union man in the colliery, and there came a time when a strike threw him— man-grown now— out of work. He had seen enough of a collier's life to know how it saps men's vitality He had made up his mind not to spend all of his life underground or over coal. And all the time the yearning for that touch of the Divine Hand was upon him, and he came to believe that some day he might preach the Gospel.

Many plans were in his mind, and he prayed over them all, this young man, strong-bodied, vigorous, thoughtful, with the air of youth in his blood. He thought of being a missionary, and when at last he settled upon the blacksmith's trade it was with the half-formed idea of going to foreign lands, and alternately working as a blacksmith and preaching.

In January, two years ago, he paid his uncle, who had a little country "smithy" at Pontardulais, $6, and bound himself as an apprentice for two years. He went to work there in his usual eager way, and in a few months had made himself of great value to the smith. But the task was not that for which he was made, and he felt it quickly.

The struggle for a decision began again until one night, when he was upon his knees over it, a great light seemed to come to him, and a new elation and a new peace. That realisation which he had sought ever since he had been a mere lad was at last his, and with it new inspiration, new joy, new hopes and purposes, and his decision was made for him almost in an instant.

He would preach; he would carry to others this message that he had heard and felt. It was near the end of his first year at the smithy, and he started at once to arrange the matter of his additional year of service with his uncle, and to plan for his new work, his life-work, that he had found at last.

The minister at Lougher in the meantime arranged for Evan Roberts to preach his first sermon one Sunday evening, and when that evening had come and passed be came to the young man and said: "You're planning to go to school, and that is right. But you're a preacher now."

During the next months, Evan Roberts was at home working at his books, for he had some examinations to pass at Newcastle-Emlen.

He had saved a little money, although he had always given to the chapel freely out of his comparatively small earnings — he received $15 a week for his work in the mines. His people were ready to deny themselves, if necessary, to help him, so that the way seemed clear for his schooling.

But while he worked hard as a student — and, of course, his

previous education had been the fragmentary, partly undirected study of a busy, ambitious young man in his leisure hours — he was much more concerned with that spiritual uplift which had suddenly obtained complete control of him.

Prayer became sustenance to him. "It means more to me than food," he said one night when he arose from his knees to answer the call to the evening meal.

And with this new life came new purpose and new vigour. He wrote religious verses in Welsh, — hymns that tried to express something of what he had within him to say, — and some of them were published and praised.

He passed his first examinations, and out of his slender purse he paid for his first term of work at the school. For a few weeks he took the stereotype courses which were mapped out for him. But the feeling came to him with growing insistence that there was other work for him to do — active work, not a few years later, but now; not as man willed, nor as he willed, but as God willed.

At last, about November 1st, almost decided, but wavering before the importance of such a decision, he heard a sermon one Sunday evening, and came from it certain that God had called him to lead a great revival in Wales.

He went home to Lougher immediately, and opened his first meetings alone, and before the doubtful eyes of those who had always known him, and who wondered at his sudden change of plan — this leaving the school which he had left them to enter only a few weeks before. He could scarcely have chosen a more difficult place to begin a difficult work.

"Where will you get the money?" asked someone.

"Money!" he cried, with that merry, boyish confidence that is part of his charm. "Never mind about the money. Look above for the money. It'll come."

At the beginning little happened. The people who came to his meetings, came out of friendliness or out of curiosity. Why should this young theological student open special meetings all unaided, and why should anyone go to hear him? And those who heard him wondered the more, for although he said little that they had not heard before, he said everything in a way that crowded conviction upon them. He told them frankly at the start that be had not prepared anything to say, but that he would only say what was put into his mind by the Holy Spirit.

Naturally, everyone talked about him, and, although few at first took him seriously, they came to hear him in gradually increasing numbers. And he seized them with a remarkable power that he had never shown before, and which he says frankly he had never felt before.

In a few days Lougher shops were closed early for the meetings; workmen hurried in late in their working clothes; evening meetings lasted far into the night; the chapel was crowded, and the road outside was lined with disappointed but waiting people. They came from miles around to hear him, and went away with old faith revived or new faith kindled. The papers began to talk of him as "a wonderful preacher"; neighbouring churches heard of him, and asked him to come to them; ministers hurried to hear him, and came away mystified at the simple power of the young man, and with a new impulse in their hearts for harder effort.

And that is the way Evan Roberts began a work which is slowly stirring the whole religious world to action.

Here is no mystic with some weird mystery to draw the morbid instincts of weak man. It is a full-blooded, hearty, young man, who has worked in the coal-mines and at the smithy, and who hammers his unambitious words home with an inspiriting vigour. Here is no dreaming sentimentalist making a weeping appeal to the sympathetic hearts of women and children. It is a deep voiced, firm-jawed young man moving men hardened by rough toil.

Here is no fiery, impassioned orator, stirring people by his rhetoric at night and being forgotten, along with his words, in the morning. It is a simple, straightforward speaker, who began alone, but who already has scores of active helpers, men and women, among those the whole course of whose lives have been changed.

Here is no exhorter terrifying his hearers into belief in God's love by threats of eternal punishment. It is a buoyant, happy man trying to show in a quiet, direct way how joyful a thing Christianity really is.

Here is no quibbler over dogmas. "You haven't any new creed in mind, have you?" I asked him one night. You don't mean to have differences with the present churches in that way?"

"Oh, no," he said in his hearty way, and with a characteristic wave of his hand. "I am merely trying to show people the love of Jesus Christ as I have experienced it."

Here is no pompous prelate who condescends to advise his congregation concerning their conduct. It is a frank, sincere man, who links his arm in yours, and means "brother" without saying it.

Here is no narrow sectarian. An army of ministers of all the denominations in Wales are working with him, and his only desire is for results.

Go into one of his meetings. Every seat is taken, there are people in the aisles, and more are crowding in. They are singing — and there is no such stirring congregational singing in the world, I believe, as in Wales — a swinging Welsh hymn, martial and inspiring.

In the midst of a verse a tall, boyish-looking young fellow slips in almost unnoticed, and takes a seat at the front, never behind the high desk, but down upon the main floor. He sings a verse with them, and perhaps starts another, while only a few realise that this is Evan Roberts.

When the singing stops, he steps out quickly before the audience, his hands in his pockets, shoulders thrown back, eyes bright, and his mouth widened in a smile.

A single sentence catches the attention of everyone in the building, for it is at once short, quiet, and vigorous. The tone is conversational, and the eyes are friendly. He begins to pace up and down, turning to the people with short, rapid phrases, and accentuating them with tense, earnest gestures as short and jerky as his speech.

He is seldom still, but when he is you can feel the restrained intensity. The movements are not those of high-strung, nervous force, but of superabundant vital energy.

Suddenly he stops short, and looks over the congregation, where every eye is upon him, and, uttering one quick sentence, laughs aloud. And such laughter as it is, boyish, joyous, confident. A moment later he is on his knees, leaning over the railing, his hands clasped, talking confidently with his audience as if it were one friend instead of many.

After a time he is on his feet again, and a Bible is in his large hands, and then he is again leaning over the railing and calling appealingly to the congregation, perhaps with tears in his eyes. Then suddenly it is over, and he sits down.

One of the girls who has come from Lougher or Pontycymmer to help him, begins to sing, and sweet as her voice is, it is not long before the congregation joins in one by one until the room rings with the melody.

He has talked less than half an hour. It has been entirely in Welsh, and yet without understanding a word he has said you have felt the spirit of it.

The frankness, the downright earnestness, the militant sincerity have given you a feeling that you have seldom had in an ordinary church service, and through the spirit of his message, they are working in the hearts of all the people about you.

And yet those who know the language say that he has said nothing that is extraordinary; that there has been little brilliancy of phrase; that he has talked simply and cheerfully of his own experience, and has asked those who are not Christians to give themselves to God.

Certainly it has all been very quiet. There has been no loud rantings, nor spectacular displays, nor open appeals to the emotions. But what is happening?

He tramps up and down the aisle, singing with the congregation, and perhaps leading them with inspiriting gestures. Now suddenly he has disappeared. In the gallery is a powerful-looking man, whose head is hidden in his arms on the back of the seat in front of him. Evan Roberts is bending over him, helping him like a brother to make the right decision.

A moment later he stands straight, his eyes flashing with joy, and cries out with joyous fervour, and then the swinging, stirring cadences of that greatest of Welsh hymns, "Diolch Iddo," which is always sung after a conversion, begins and grows in volume until they sweep another man upon his feet with an avowal of his changed life.

Evan Roberts is once more before the people, and he breaks in upon the singing with a few half-spoken, half-whispered words. A wave of deep feeling dashes aside something of his self-control as he begs them to "Come to Him! Come to Him!" and he sinks upon his knees in prayer, while one of the girls who have come with him sings a simple hymn in English.

Slowly the congregation has risen out of itself, out of its curiosity, out of its indifference. Something has caught them as in a rushing tide, and is bearing them on resistlessly. A minister rises as the song ends, and declares that, although he has preached the Gospel for years, he is now for the first time a Christian. There are others waiting to follow him now, men and women, some of whom have been negative Christians, and some of whom have never professed any religion.

Now it is a man who is known to the community chiefly as a drunkard; now it is a man whom you heard scoffing outside at the meeting and the missioner; now it is a woman who tremblingly whispers a few inaudible words, and sinks back into her seat; now it is a young lad of twenty, who has come out of curiosity, and will go out determined to a new, purposeful life.

Evan Roberts is everywhere — now upon his knees beside a man in the last seat by the door; now talking in his quiet, triumphant way from half-way down the aisle; now standing before them all as a burly man rises in the gallery, and telling him with closed eyes that he seems to see God on high confessing the man, even as the man is now confessing his God.

And always he is dominant, masterful, cheery, quiet, his power growing with his tense eagerness and his tremendous earnestness.

A cynical, indifferent critic watching any one of these meetings would be forced to admit that the young man is sincere to the core; that he descends to no trick of gesture or word or act; that he is straightforward and simple to the last degree; that he does not try to force people against their will, and yet that in some way he draws all before him, not to himself, but to the Spirit of Whom he is the avowed disciple.

And, in spite of himself, this hardened critic will feel the impulse and will say to himself, as a tough, knotty-looking man said to me in the train today: "There must be something in it." And by that admission he does what Evan Roberts wishes him to do — he forgets the speaker, the mere agent, and reaches for that lifting Hand to which the missioner is trying to lead everyone he meets, and to whom he talks.

Go to Evan Roberts outside of a meeting if you can find an opportunity between the sessions that begin in the morning, and continue in the afternoon, and again at night, and last until early in the morning again, with only a brief hour for hurried meals; meetings that are sometimes held in three different towns in one day, with a considerable railway journey between each.

Go to him, I say, and talk with him. He is exactly the same man you have seen in the chapel, the same tense, manly man of the sort who grow upon one, and who are more admirable the closer one is to them.

"What is your message?" I asked him one quiet Sunday noon, as we were on our way to enjoy the whole-souled hospitality of a rugged Welshman and his kindly wife. He had locked his arm in mine, and his face beamed with "goodwill towards men." He half-stopped as if to poise his thoughts.

"It's very simple," he said, with a quaint Welsh accent that makes his English very attractive.

"I have found what I believe to be the highest kind of Christianity. I want to give my life, God helping me, to lead others, many others, to find it. Many have found it already, thank God, and they are doing what I am doing, in a large or little way, as God gives them light. And that is all there is to the revival, and all there is to me, my friend."

He had spoken slowly, as if weighing the words. He paused for a second, and then throwing all his pent-up feelings into a single exclamation, in a way that gives complete conviction of the man's utter sincerity and abandonment of itself.

"Oh," he cried in a long breath, his eyes bright with happiness, "it is great. I have always wanted to do this, but I didn't know it, I wasn't sure of it till God showed me the way."

There is no such thing as evasion in him. If he likes what is said by someone else he says so, and shows it frankly. If he is not interested he shows his indifference with the same sincerity. His tongue is not a loose one, and he is slow to talk of himself or of the work he himself is doing, but the spirit of the man is as boundless as his energy, as determined as his confidence. He is a Welshman, and proud of it.

He loves his own language, and laughed his inspiring, boyish laugh often at my clumsy attempts to speak the words and phrases he put into my mouth. He goes upstairs, and I can hear him talking vigorously with another man of about his own age, who a few weeks ago came to his meetings, and who is now one of his most helpful assistants. He ran up the stairs, and he comes running down, singing at the top of his deep, resonant, bass voice.

"My voice is all right today," he cries, with his merry laugh. "Last night it was bad, but it was given to me again to-day for my work."

The short respite is ended, and we start back for another meeting at a different chapel. He strides along, stopping now and then to speak to people in the many groups that are walking down the middle of the road — as they usually do in Wales — towards the same destination. Up every hilly side street they came, and they do not hold themselves aloof from him as if he were different and greater than they.

It would be difficult for anyone to hold himself aloof from this buoyant, simple, honest young man, who is working with them, not over them; who is leading them, not from some comfortable seat at the rear, or in some place of glory before them, but by their side, helpfully, mightily.

I watch that swinging, tall, big-boned figure, his decisive gesture, his firm jaw and steady, smiling mouth, and the fire of youth and of religious consecration in his eyes. I hear the resounding laughter and see the flash of clear, even teeth under his lips.

I feel the unassuming simplicity, the boyish ingenuousness, the commanding sincerity, and see how at one he is with the people, catching a hand here and grasping an arm or shoulder there in open -hearted friendliness, carrying his enthusiasm, his confidence, his dominating, cheerful spirit into their hearts. And inevitably I say to myself: "Here is a true 'sky-pilot,' who knows the course and who is giving himself that others may learn it."

It was said to me that he was not resourceful enough; that he has not had enough education; that he is naïve, untrained, a mere boy. It may be so, and some of this is, of course, evidently true. But I never knew a man to whom education added kindness, or goodness, or fervour, or strength of soul; resourcefulness often becomes cunning. The Apostles of the New Testament were, some of them, humble fishermen who became "fishers of men."

Remember that this young man of twenty-six, in the freshness of his zeal and with absolutely honest unselfish purpose, gave up his schooling and, all alone, began to hold meetings under no auspices except that of the Spirit which was with him.

And that in a few rapid weeks he lifted all South Wales upon a wave of religious thought and feeling; that he has turned hundreds of lives that were well-nigh useless into great usefulness and unmeasured happiness, beside bringing a new life into thousands of other hearts and lives; that he, a Methodist in training but under no denominational leading strings, has brought together all the Nonconformist churches of that section into a solid phalanx working for single, simple purpose.

All men honour the convictions and the strength of a real man. This is a real man. And he has an added Power which men can feel but cannot fathom.

There is a simple hymn that is sung in revival meetings in America that typifies the spirit of Evan Roberts' revival in Wales. "There is sunshine in my soul." A preacher in Swansea is reported to have said that, although he had not attended any of the meetings, he had read about them in the papers, and he added that he considered the appeals "barbarous."

If this preacher ever hears Evan Roberts, and I hope he will, he will be ashamed of himself; for Roberts talks chiefly of God's love and of the great joy of living in obedience to that love. As to his appeal, it is simple and direct, and is seldom characterised by a great demand upon his hearers' emotions.

None of the hundreds of dramatic scenes that have occurred in these meetings have come while Roberts has been talking. They have come afterwards, and often a considerable time afterwards. And Evan Roberts, I believe, has said that he is glad that this is the case, for it proves that it is not Roberts, the man, his magnetism, or his personality that is so great an influence, but rather the Spirit at work in the meetings.

A few times, indeed, so greatly has he been moved by his own strong feeling, he has lost control of himself and has broken down in the midst of his appeal.

"But I mustn't do that," he said to me frankly. "It has a mere emotional appeal, and its effect is temporary and does not do the good I want to do. I don't wish to move men temporarily. I want to convince them permanently. But the Spirit will guide me."

He has something of the same feeling about the hymn singing, I am told. Much as he loves it himself, and music is in him to his very fingertips, he feels — I judge both from the hearsay and from watching him break into the midst of the singing when, in a way they have in Wales, they repeat over and over the same stirring melody — that too much singing moves only surface emotions and takes the congregations' mind from the deeper influence of prayer and close communion with God. He believes completely in the efficacy of prayer, and he has for many years spent a considerable amount of time daily upon his knees.

Indeed, one of the great differences between this revival and some others is the comparative quietness of method, if it can be called method. The "sunshine" of it is another. There is nothing spectacular about the man or about any of his helpers.

His talk is simple and forcible; the young women converts who sing, sing simple, appealing hymns that suggest the happiness of Christianity; and I saw day after day an entire audience caught in the spell of the fresh young voices' sweetness and the tenderness of the songs' sentiment, and the evident feeling of the young singers who were using the best means they had been given to add their message to his, until there was scarcely anyone whose eyes were not wet, and yet many eyes saw some things the clearer for the sudden mist.

And if some of the local ministers are too zealous occasionally in trying to force those who are least moved, that is not part of Evan Roberts' intention, and it only serves to show how ministers as well as people have been seized by his impelling force.

What Evan Roberts has done, and is doing, seems wonderful when one remembers how this revival began, and how it has grown; but the man's confidence, not in himself, nor in any human power he has, but in the guidance of a Spirit from above is boundless.

"If you can do this in a few weeks," I asked him one day, "what will you do in a lifetime?"

"We'll change the world," he cried, and his face was aglow with the joy of his hopes. "We'll change the world. I believe it."

Do not think that he meant this as a boast, for he did not, nor as personal pride in his achievements. It is only his entire trust that the whole world will be brought to God, and his belief that he will be one of the forces by which men will be converted to that new life that means everything to him. And, indeed, his success elsewhere can scarcely be more surprising than what he has already done.

"Will you go to London?" I asked him more than a month ago. "Certainly you will finish the work here first."

"I have already had three invitations to London," he said. "I shall go whenever the Spirit guides me, but I should rather work here now."

When Roberts leaves a town he leaves often one or two young converts, and some of the young women whose singing at his meetings began naturally as a result of their new religious experience. And in this way the movement is not dropped suddenly when he goes, but continues while he travels on to spread it elsewhere.

Ministers, too, who have caught the fire from him, go back to their churches in places where Roberts has not yet been heard, and begin more meetings. So great has become the demand upon his time, that one preacher has taken from him all the worry of plans, and is arranging his itinerary, and is seeing to all the details of his movements.

"I believe it's merely a money-making affair," said a man, scoffing at the revival in the hall of a mining town hotel. And that reminds us of the question Evan Roberts was asked at Lougher when he began his meetings: "Where will the money come from?"

I have attended a number of his meetings and I have not seen a collection taken, although I believe there have been collections to defray travelling expenses.

But railroad fares are not large in that country where the mining towns are only a few miles apart, and the churches where he speaks can afford to pay these, and to entertain him and those who come with him, at their homes. And this is all Evan Roberts is concerned with, to get enough money to carry on the work.

There have been religious charlatans, commercial prophets in both senses and with both spellings, but this is not one. He is seeking honestly not money or personal fame, but the glory of God. I say, not fame, or notoriety. The man would scarcely talk with me when I told him frankly I was a journalist.

"I do not care for interviews," he said quickly. And it was only when he realized how the true story of what is happening in Wales might stir the religious thought and feeling of men the world over that he made free to talk.

Perhaps there is no better example of a town which has both felt the thrill of revival interest, and which has continued its results long after the first impulse died away, than Aberdare.

Evan Roberts was still at Lougher in the midst of his most crowded meetings, where he worked day and night, slept little, ate little, and threw his entire vitality into his new achievement.

It so happened that the Methodist preacher at Trecynon, on the edge of Aberdare, sent word one week that he could not occupy the chapel pulpit on the following Sunday.

In that country many of the preachers are itinerant to a greater or less degree, preaching in one chapel a certain number of times and spending the remainder of their time doing the same work elsewhere. The people of the little church had little time in which to find a substitute.

Someone, however, had heard that the man named Evan Roberts, who was said to be doing remarkable things at Lougher, was a fine preacher as well as a revivalist. At the last moment they wrote, asking him to speak at Trecynon on Sunday, and received an answer that he would come.

Sunday morning at church time no preacher appeared, and it was not until the congregation had waited drearily, spasmodically singing hymns, for a long time, that a young man, with a springy step and an entire lack of gloomy solemnity, came in with five young women, and, to their surprise, made his way to the front.

For a half hour he talked to them in his characteristic way, saying more or less conventional things in a way that somehow gripped their hearts and made them sit straight and then lean forward, so as not to lose either a word or a particle of that enthusiastic spirit.

Then some of the girls who had come with him sang, and the coldness of the people was half melted as they joined in and sang with Welsh voices and Welsh fervor.

Evan Roberts stopped at Trecynon during the week, carrying on the same sort of work with the same inspiring, hearty zeal that had brought all Lougher to the Moriah Chapel. And, as at Lougher, men came to scoff at the "boy-preacher who saw visions," and before they left their first meeting had given their lives to Christian work.

All the churches were at work quickly, and religious power swept over the town like a mighty wind. People went to hear Evan Roberts, and stayed to drop to their knees before God.

All sorts of men and women, from Tom Hughes, the atheist, to young girls whose lives were waiting for a hand to mould them, stood up before crowded pews and told, with a simple eloquence that no one at Aberdare knew they possessed, what new, bright light had come to them.

One hardy miner, who had gone out of curiosity, came out hurriedly at about eleven o'clock and went home and to bed. Shortly after midnight he arose, dressed himself, and went back to the meeting to cry out that God had saved him, and that he couldn't sleep until he had declared publicly for Him.

And then, when the people were filling three good-sized chapels every night, and when, far down toward the centre, people standing still in the clear, quiet, moonlit night, heard the martial swing of their triumphal hymns, and, wondering, felt, even there, the stir that was in the air; when dozens of men's lives and women's lives were being changed every day, remade in determination at least in a few hours, Evan Roberts went away because he was needed more elsewhere. His brother, Dan Roberts, however, came in his place.

I attended two meetings there, weeks after Evan Roberts had gone. One afternoon, just outside the little chapel in Roberts' town, across the railroad from Trecynon, I met an elderly Englishman who had just left the meeting.

"I was afraid I'd never feel that way again," he said to me, "but I have now. I've been through three pretty strong revivals, but I never was moved in my life as I was this afternoon. I haven't been so happy since I was a boy." There were tears in his eyes, but his mouth was smiling joyously. I left him standing there looking up at the sunset light about the high hills, and blessing God in his heart.

Within was a strange scene. It was all disorder. About the altar-rail knelt a line of people praying for forgiveness.

Directly before me one of the Christian Endeavour workers was sitting with his arm about a man who was evidently just from work, whose head was sunk upon his arms, and whose great body was shaking with emotion, while his friend chanted to him in low, almost uncanny monotony "the old, old story." At the left a young lad of twenty, his eyes closed, his face upturned with a rapt look, was talking in high, loud voice, rapidly, confidently, although until three days before he had always feared to talk before people, even a few, casually.

In the gallery the largest, strongest-looking man in the room had thrown himself forward and was sobbing in his hands; while a little, sad-faced woman and a sturdy, apple-cheeked girl — his wife and daughter probably — put their arms about him as if to drag him on to better things. Behind, a little man with a large voice was singing alone one of the less familiar Welsh hymns, and he seemed entirely oblivious of the crowds about him. All this was happening just as I went in.

Now a quaint, pitiful little figure in black kneels, and in quavering words, scarcely above a whisper, begs that her boy may be brought to God; and then a hush falls upon nearly all as a young man comes hurrying up the aisles, self-conscious, but with his jaw set tightly, and kneels down beside her. Then her arms grope their way about his broad shoulders, and until after I have left the chapel they remain there, mother and son, in tears and happiness.

Meanwhile the audience bursts quickly into that stirring, swinging hymn that follows conversion — music that, I think, caught me in its sweeping melody with more resistless power than any song and any singing I have ever heard.

To me no oratorio society, no group of trained professional singers that it has been my good fortune to hear, sing as well as almost anyone of the Welsh congregations I heard sing at the Roberts meetings, and here and there were wonderful individual voices, backed by great musical temperament.

Suddenly, as the long hymn ends, the little woman and the young girl beside the man in the gallery leap to their feet in joy and wave their hands. Again the triumphant hymn, louder, now rumbling bass and strong tenor weighing evenly with the simple but mighty air. In all this time I have not heard a word from any of the three ministers, except the usual expressions of joy and the picturesque Welsh words of encouragement.

And this is another way in which the Roberts meetings differ from any other revival meetings I have attended.

The people are the meeting, not the preacher, once his short talk is ended, though his spirit remains to fire them to congregational rather than individual leadership.

The evening meeting was similar, and lasted far into the morning, a joyful meeting with its greatest enthusiasm just before it closed. This was a month after Evan Roberts first stirred the Aberdare people, and suggests that he stirred not merely the surface but the depths. And it is the same elsewhere.

The stories that might be told of the experiences, the deeds, and the sayings of individuals among the congregations in the Welsh revival — dramatic scenes, of tender pathos, lightning bits of humour — are already numbered in thousands and tens of thousands. And each one has served as added fuel to this religious flame, which, like the fires that sometimes have swept the prairies and the forests of the Western States, has gone beyond the power of men to stop, and must determine its own destiny.

Every night and every morning they are repeated in the mines and the shops, on the streets, and in the tidy little homes of Wales. The newspapers bear them on where Evan Roberts is only a name, and a single vital incident often carries the spark which sets new fires burning fiercely.

A clergyman, so one story goes, is standing in the open street with a collier. They have just come from a meeting.

"A good meeting," says the clergyman, "afire with enthusiasm. But what will happen when the fuel is exhausted?"

"Fuel," cries the Welshman "No fear of Wales running out of

fuel. You'll be an archbishop before this light goes out." And then
and there he raises his voice in prayer for the doubting clergyman.

Up in Ebenezer Chapel at Trecynon at midnight comes a well-
known man, and the people stop singing and stare at him in amazement. He is an atheist. "I have burned my books that said there was
no God," he says. "I was shipwrecked and the waves were gathering fast about the plank which alone stood between me and hell.
But God called to me and I came to Him and was lifted out of de-
struction." Tom Hughes, the atheist, knows what he means when he
sings "Throw out the life-line."

A certain collier in Cilfynydd has been "cropped" for "filling
dirty coal." In anger and with threats he tells the officials that he
will make trouble for them. He'll have it taken up by the union, and
the union will make the officials understand what they can do and
what they can't do. He goes to hear Evan Roberts, and he comes
from the meeting in a totally new spirit.

"I'm not going to say anything to the union," he tells the officials, "and I'll go back to work. And what's more, you won't have
to talk about dirty coal in my trams again."

"We've prayed for this awakening," cries a workman at one
meeting. "We've seen the devil's worst often; but now, at last, we
are seeing Christ's best."

A certain gambler is owed £100. After one meeting he goes to a
clergyman and offers to give money to the church and to the cause.

"I can't take gambling money," says the preacher as gently as
possible.

The gambler is bitterly disappointed. He has no money except
"gambling money." He goes away and refuses the £100 owed him
as a gambling debt.

A young woman trembling with emotion rises at Pontycymmer.
Everyone knows her. Only a short time ago she was a leading figure in the police-court. "Can anyone as bad as I am be saved?" she
asks. "Certainly," cries the missioner. "No one of us is too bad to
be saved." Tears roll down the woman's cheek. "No one has fallen
lower than I have," she declares. "He saves me. Come to Him, all
the rest of you," Is it a wonder that people all about her, who have

sins of their own, and hesitate to confess them, are weeping, or that the whole audience is suddenly moved.

Throughout this section of Wales in every town there are clubs formed for men. Ostensibly they are for social intercourse, but in reality, as far as I have been able to learn, many of them are little more than select drinking places, and houses where the members can evade the law against public drinking on Sundays.

Listen to these two confessions at Ammanford. The first is from a middle-aged man holding a baby in his arms: "I used to spend three or four pounds in a single evening at the bar. I'd give my wife and children a few stray shillings now and then. I'd steal coppers from my child's money-box and spend them for beer. I was seldom sober. But, thank God, that's done with."

Another man follows him quickly when he sits down: "I've been the worst kind of a drunkard," he says. "And what's more — and this is something my wife here never knew until now — I served three years in jail as a professional thief. Now I am really happy for the first time in my life."

A farmer near Lougher, it was said, in the early days of the revival, sent one of his men with a load of turnips to the town. This man had been converted to a new life at one of the first meetings. On the way to Lougher a woman met him and begged him to join her in prayers for her husband.

The man left his cart and went with her. An hour later the farmer, coming by, discovered the cart standing by the wayside and watched over by two children. Inquiring the way to the house, he followed the servant and in a few moments he, too, was kneeling in prayer beside his servant and the good woman.

One man, a workman, asked where he was going by some of his friends, remarked with a laugh that he was going down to see that "crazy-man," Evan Roberts. Before the meeting was over he had risen, trembling, to his feet and had asked the people to pray for him.

Here is a seafaring man telling of a wreck from which he was saved by a life-line, and the entire congregation throws itself unrestrainedly into the hymn, "Throw out the life-line."

Here are a pugilist giving up his "profession," a postman getting leave of absence to attend meetings, a policeman remarking that people are going mad over the revival, and then after attending one meeting joining the "mad people" at whom he jeered, a racing man burning his racing clothes, a notorious "rough" asking prayers for his "pals," a girl throwing her arms about another girl whom she had refused to speak to for a year, a school at which prayer meetings have temporarily replaced some of the study, and colliers working in the pits kneeling in prayer beside their trams.

These only suggest the changes in men's hearts and lives that are being made by the tens of thousands in Wales. What is doing it? Come to Ynishir. A chapel is well filled with expectant people. They are singing Welsh hymns as they wait the coming of the missioner of whom they have heard so much, and whom they have never seen. Now and then some fervent church-member, who until Evan Roberts began to stir the churches went about his religious duties with little life or animation, prays in chanting monotone for the Spirit to descend upon this meeting, or quotes with gentle voice "The Lord is my Shepherd," — I heard a dozen men do this at various meetings, — or rises to his feet and, one hand raised while the other covers his eyes, tells what God has done for him.

They are singing again when Evan Roberts comes in quietly, listening with a happy smile on his lips to the swelling tide of melody. Up in the gallery there is a group of young people and children and unconsciously they are leading the singing with their fresh young voices. Roberts' eyes, wandering keenly about the room and, to use a figure, shaking hands with every other pair of eyes they meet, light upon these enthusiastic children and his smile broadens.

I could listen to such singing all night," he declares when the fifth "repeat" has been finished. And again the music rises triumphantly.

"Mae'r etifeddiaeth i ni'n d'od,
Wrth Destament ein Tad."

A moment later the missioner is talking in his jerky, whole-hearted, inspiring way, with the hymn as a text, saying simple, pithy things that appeal strongly to the people before him. Suddenly he turns to the children in the gallery.

"Will you go out into the streets of Ynishire and sing that hymn there as you have sung it here?"

There is immediate and inspiring response.

"If you will," cries the missioner, his face alight, "the people here must be hard if they don't yearn for Christ as they listen."

The meeting goes on. Miss Rees is talking in Welsh now, and singing in English that simple hymn, with its catching melody, in which all can join:

"Looking this way, yes, looking this way,
Loved ones are waiting, looking this way."

Now Mr. Roberts is calling beseechingly to the people to stand up for God.

"'He that is not with me is against me.' Where do you, each of you, stand. Are you for Him or against Him. Be men and tell us."

No one could describe or explain how the climax has come, but here it is. Gradually the pool of human hearts has been stirred deeper and yet deeper, and now the flood of confession, of contrition, of penitence for the past, of aspiration for better things, bursts out in every part of the hall. There are men on their feet and women on their knees all about us, talking freely of what they have done, of what they have been, and of what they mean to do and be; or praying plaintively for forgiveness for themselves and for those who are dear to them.

"Diolch Iddo," "Thanks to Him," rolls out a mighty chorus.

Come to Ferndale. Trehondda Chapel is filled with all sorts of people, all creeds and no creed, many grades of education and no education. Already the indefinable stir that we have seen grow so often and so inexplicably has begun.

Evan Roberts speaks: "Let us see what God's Spirit will do for us in a quiet meeting. It did wonderful things at Lougher when no one sung or spoke."

A few moments later all are kneeling in five minutes of silent prayer. The crowded room is still except for quick gasps of sobbing breath from those who are deeply moved. Here and there a half audible voice is mumbling inarticulate prayer. Deeper yet grows the silence and more impressive. Wrinkled faces are upturned, and unseeing eyes look upward. Heads are bowed in folded hands. Shoulders are convulsed with emotion, and lips are moving from which no sound comes.

Still the preacher gives no sign. Gradually a single low voice is heard in all parts of the chapel, singing sweetly the hymn, "Have you seen Him?" in Welsh. For an instant there is the stillness of listening with bated breath; then slowly other voices join in singing until the building rings with thrilling melody. It is as if they have burst from prayer into song.

And this is a scene of the revival which so respected a paper as the Lancet, evidently without investigating it except through the reports of the sensational papers and its own prejudice, calls "a debauch of emotionalism," "a hysterical outburst," marked with "scenes of disorder."

Come to Treorky. We shall have great difficulty in getting into this meeting unless we are very early. So great is the interest that the football game in the afternoon has been played before an assemblage that was only three or four times the size of the team in the field.

A man stops us outside and points to the packed vestibule and the waiting, disappointed people outside. "That's the most remarkable thing I ever saw," he says. "It's the first time I ever saw a church where they had to hang out a 'standing room only' sign. Most always you can occupy a whole row in the stalls free, and here I'd pay a guinea for a seat and I can't get it! It's amazing, that's what it is, amazing."

He talks like a theatrical man, and he is evidently a stranger for anyone who has attended Evan Roberts' meetings knows that this is the rule and not the exception wherever he has gone. He turns away before we make any appreciable impression upon the almost solid wall of people standing at the door, and goes off down the street shaking his head.

Evan Roberts is already speaking when we have worked our way to a place where we can hear. He is talking pleadingly, with manly pathos and deep feeling, about the agony of our Saviour. As he talks we seem to see the picture of Him in the Garden of Gethsemane, and to understand something of His suffering.

Suddenly a sweet, girlish voice breaks in on the missioner's quick speech. The words are Welsh, but the voice is tense with emotion, and the liquid sweetness of it holds the entire congregation taut and motionless.

The verse ends and the speaker proceeds with his moving description. Suddenly the voice breaks in again. It is Annie Davies. We can see her now.

The words are Welsh still, but we have heard them so often that we understand them. "Jesus only," sings the thrilling voice, and stops short. Her hands cover her eyes and the girl is sobbing unrestrainedly. "Oh, Jesu, Jesu," she moans, "for me." There is a moment of silence, broken only by pent-up sobbing. Now the entire congregation is singing, and singing mightily, and there are tears in our eyes. And we have come merely as onlookers.

Whether his share in the work be great or little, I think Evan Roberts cares as little as any human person can care, so long as the work is done. No one of all those who have watched him more closely and continuously than I have, have seen a single sign of any tendency in him to place himself ahead of any of his co-workers. The people have done that, and he accepts the large opportunity gladly.

Personally, I think I have never met a man who appealed to me as being so completely consecrated to his cause as this young man of twenty-six years, trained in the colliery and at the "smithy." When one thinks of it, no young man of his years and native environment could have endured against so strong a tide of personal success unless he had an enduring grip upon mighty moorings.

3: The Lessons Of The Revival

"For these are not drunken, as ye suppose, seeing it is but the third hour of the day; but this is that which hath been spoken by the prophet Joel:

> And it shall be in the last days, saith God,
> I will pour forth of My Spirit upon all flesh:
> And your sons and your daughters shall prophesy,
> And your young men shall see visions,
> And your old men shall dream dreams:
> Yea, and on My bond-servants and on My bond-maidens in those days
> Will I pour forth of My Spirit, and they shall prophesy."
> Acts ii. 15 - 18.

I HAVE not read these words as a text, but as an introduction to what I desire to say, as God shall help me, concerning the most recent manifestation of the Pentecostal power. I refer to the great work of God that is going on in Wales at this time; and I trust that something more than curiosity makes you desire to hear of this work, for I am not speaking with any intention to satisfy curiosity. I want now in the simplest way to speak to you, first, very briefly, and as far as it is possible, of what my own eyes have seen, my own ears heard, and my own heart felt.

I do this in order that we may ask finally, What are the lessons God would teach us in this day of His visitation? Yet I cannot help reverting, before going further, to the passage that I have read in your hearing. Peter stood in the midst of one of the most wonderful scenes that the world has ever beheld. When men said of the shouting multitude that they were drunk, Peter said, "No, these men are not drunken as ye suppose;" but "this is that" which was spoken by the Prophet Joel.

If anyone shall say to me, "What do you think of the Welsh revival? " I say at once, "This is that."

This is no mere piece of imagination, and it certainly is not a piece of exaggeration. "I will pour forth of My Spirit upon all flesh, and your sons and your daughters shall prophesy," is the promise now evidently fulfilled in Wales. If you ask for proof of that assertion I point to the signs. "Your young men shall see visions!" That is exactly what is happening. It does not at all matter that this cynical and dust-covered age laughs at the vision. The young men are seeing it. "And your old men shall dream dreams," and that is happening. The vision goes forward, the dream goes backward; and the old men are dreaming of '59, and feeling its thrill again. "Yea, and on My bond-servants and on My hand-maidens," that is, on the slaves and the domestic servants, "I will pour My Spirit in those days; and they shall prophesy." It does not at all matter that some regular people are objecting to the irregular doings. "This is that." If you ask me the meaning of the Welsh Revival, I say, it is Pentecost Continued, without one single moment's doubt.

PENTECOST CONTINUED

But, for a few moments let me speak of the thing itself. Let me talk familiarly and quietly, as though sitting in my own room.

I left London on Monday, reaching Cardiff at 8:30 that evening, and my friend who met me said to me, "What are you going to do? Will you go home, or will you go to the meeting?" I said, "What meeting?" He said, "There is a meeting in Roath Road Chapel." "Oh," I said, "I would rather have a meeting than home." We went. The meeting had been going on an hour and a half when we got there, and we stayed for two hours and a half, and went home, and the meeting was still going on, and I had not then touched what is spoken of as — it is not my phrase, but it is expressive — the "fire zone." I was on the outskirts of the work. It was a wonderful night, utterly without order, characterised from first to last by the orderliness of the Spirit of God.

But it is of Tuesday that I would specially speak. I was the whole of that day in Clydach Vale, spending eight hours in the actual meetings and the rest of the time in the company of Evan Roberts, whom God has so wonderfully raised up. When I had been to the evening meeting on Tuesday I told him I would not come back on Wednesday, for reasons to be stated hereafter. Let me only say now in passing that I am perfectly convinced that we had better keep our hands off this work. I will explain that more fully presently. On Wednesday we returned to Cardiff and, in answer to an invitation, Mr. Gregory Mantle and I took a meeting in this Roath Road Wesleyan Chapel, and on Thursday we took three meetings, spending seven hours there.

I want to speak of the Tuesday only. It was my holy privilege to come into the centre of this wonderful work and movement. Arriving in the morning in the village, everything seemed quiet, and we wended our way to the place where a group of chapels stood. Oh, these chapels through Wales! Thank God for them! And everything was so quiet and orderly that we had to ask where the meeting was. And a lad, pointing to a chapel, said, "In there." Not a single person outside. Everything was quiet. We made our way through the open door, and just managed to get inside, and found the chapel crowded from floor to ceiling with a great mass of people. What was the occupation of the service? It is impossible for me to tell you finally and fully. Suffice it to say that throughout that service there was singing and praying, and personal testimony, but no preaching. The only break in upon the evidently powerful continuity of the service was when some one in the meeting, who happened to know me, said that they would like to hear me speak. And that is why I decided never to go again into these meetings.

WHY I DECIDED NEVER TO GO AGAIN

For the moment the thoughts of the meeting were turned toward me there was a break in the continuity and the power. If it were possible for me in any way to disguise myself I would go back again, and get back into the middle of the movement, but I am afraid it is a little too late in the day for that. Of course I did not move to speak, but when, presently, it was evident that there was this break, I rose and spoke a few words, urging them not to allow the presence of any stranger to divert their attention, and the meeting moved on, and I was allowed to hide myself again. It was a meeting characterised by a perpetual series of interruptions and disorderliness. It was a meeting characterised by a great continuity and an absolute order.

You say, "How do you reconcile these things?" I do not reconcile them. They are both there. I leave you to reconcile them. If you put a man into the midst of one of these meetings who knows nothing of the language of the Spirit, and nothing of the life of the Spirit, one of two things will happen to him. He will either pass out saying, "These men are drunk," or he himself will be swept up by the fire into the Kingdom of God. If you put a man down who knows the language of the Spirit, he will be struck by this most peculiar thing. I am speaking with diffidence, for I have never seen anything like it in my life; while a man praying is disturbed by the breaking out of song, there is no sense of disorder, and the prayer merges into song, and back into testimony, and back again into song for hour after hour, without guidance. These are the three occupations — singing, prayer, testimony. Evan Roberts was not present. There was no human leader.

Mr. Mantle was with me, and spoke a word or two, when a man in the gallery rose and said to him in broken English, "Is your work in London near Greenwich?" "Yes," said Mr. Mantle, "close to Greenwich." "Take this address down," said the man, "my brother is there. He is drinking and a sceptic. I am praying for him." Mr. Mantle pulled out his note-book and said, "Give me the address," and he dictated it to him, and then they started singing "Songs of Praises," and the man prayed, and Mr. Mantle is on his track today. That is an incident. A most disorderly proceeding, you say? I will be very glad when that happens here, when you will break through all conventionalities. When a man is in agony about the soul of his brother, he will dare to ask. But it must only be as the spontaneous answer of the soul to the Spirit of God.

In the afternoon we were at another chapel, and another meeting, equally full, and this time Evan Roberts was present.

EVAN ROBERTS WAS PRESENT

He came into the meeting when it had been on for an hour and a half. I went with him, and with the utmost difficulty we reached the platform. I took absolutely no part, and he took very little part. He spoke, but his address — if it could be called an address — was punctuated perpetually by song and prayer and testimony. And Evan Roberts works on that plan, never hindering anyone. As the result of that afternoon I venture to say that if that address Evan Roberts gave in broken fragments had been reported, the whole of it could have been read in six or seven minutes. As the meeting went on, a man rose in the gallery and said, "So and So," naming some man, "has decided for Christ," and then in a moment the song began. They did not sing "Songs of Praises" they sang "Diolch Iddo," and the weirdness and beauty of it swept over the audience. It was a song of praise because that man was born again. There are no enquiry rooms, no penitent forms, but some worker announces, or an enquirer openly confesses Christ, the name is registered, and the song breaks out, and they go back to testimony and prayer.

In the evening exactly the same thing. I can tell you no more, save that I personally stood for three solid hours wedged so that I could not lift my hands at all. That which impressed me most was the congregation. I looked along the gallery of the chapel on my right, and there were three women, and the rest were men packed solidly in. If you could but for once have seen the men, evidently colliers, with the blue seam that told of their work on their faces, clean and beautiful. Beautiful, did I say? Many of them lit with heaven's own light, radiant with the light that never was on sea and land. Great rough, magnificent, poetic men by nature, but the nature had slumbered long. To-day it is awakened, and I looked on many a face, and I knew that men did not see me, did not see Evan Roberts, but they saw the face of God and the eternities. I left that evening, after having been in the meeting three hours, at 10. 30, and it swept on, packed as it was, until an early hour next morning, song and prayer and testimony and conversion and confession of sin by leading church members publicly, and the putting of it away, and all the while no human leader, no one indicating the next thing to do, no one checking the spontaneous movement.

Now, for one moment let me go a step further and speak just a word or two about the man himself.

THE MAN HIMSELF

Evan Roberts is hardly more than a boy, simple and natural, no orator, no leader of men; nothing of the masterfulness that characterized such men as Wesley, and Whitefield, and Moody; no leader of men. One of the most brilliant writers in one of our morning papers said of Evan Roberts, in a tone of sorrow, that he lacked the qualities of leadership, and the writer said if but some prophet; did now arise he could sweep everything before him. God has not chosen that a prophet shall arise. It is quite true. Evan Roberts is no orator, no leader. What is he? I mean now with regard to this great movement. He is the mouthpiece of the fact that there is no human guidance as to man or organization. The burden of what he says to the people is this: it is not man, do not wait for me, depend on God, obey the Spirit. But whenever moved to do so, he speaks under the guidance of the Spirit. His work is not that of appealing to men so much as that of creating an atmosphere by calling men to follow the guidance of the Spirit in whatever the Spirit shall say to them.

I do not hesitate to say that God has set His hand upon the lad, beautiful in simplicity, ordained in his devotion, lacking all the qualities that we have looked for in preachers, and prophets, and leaders. He has put him in the forefront of this movement that the world may see that He does choose the things that are not to bring

to nought the things that are, the weak things of the world to confound the things that are mighty; a man who lacks all the essential
qualities which we say make for greatness, in order that through
him in simplicity and power He may move to victory.

For a moment let us stand back, and look at the whole thing
more generally. Let me speak of some of the incidental peculiarities.

PECULIARITIES OF THE MOVEMENT

as I saw it, and gathered information concerning it on the
ground. In connection with the Welsh revival there is no preaching,
no order, no hymnbooks, no choirs, no organs, no collections, and,
finally, no advertising. Now, think of that for a moment, again, will
you? Think of all our work. I am not saying these things are wrong.
I simply want you to see what God is doing. There were the organs,
but silent; the ministers, but among the rest of the people, rejoicing
and prophesying with the rest, only there was no preaching. Yet the
Welsh revival is the revival of preaching to Wales. Everybody is
preaching. No order, and yet it moves from day to day, week to
week, county to county, with matchless precision, with the order of
an attacking force. No books, but, ah me, I nearly wept to-night
over the singing of our last hymn. Mr. Stead was asked if he
thought the revival would spread to London, and he said, "It depends upon whether you can sing." He was not so wide of the
mark. When these Welshmen sing, they sing the words like men
who believe them. They abandon themselves to their singing. We
sing as though we thought it would not be respectable to be heard
by the man next to us. No choir, did I say? It was all choir. And
hymns! I stood and listened in wonder and amazement as that congregation on that night sang hymn after hymn, long hymns, sung
through without hymnbooks. Oh, don't you see it? The Sunday
school is having its harvest now. The family altar is having its harvest now. The teaching of hymns and the Bible among those Welsh
hills and valleys is having its harvest now. No advertising. The
whole thing advertises itself. You tell me the Press is advertising it.
I tell you they did not begin advertising until the thing caught fire

and spread. And let me say to you, one of the most remarkable things is the attitude of the Welsh Press. I come across instance after instance of men converted by reading the story of the revival in the Western Mail and the South Wale: Daily News.

WHAT IS THE ORIGIN OF THE MOVEMENT?

In the name of God let us all cease trying to find it. At least let us cease trying to trace it to any one man or convention. You cannot trace it, and yet I will trace it tonight. Whence has it come? All over Wales — I am giving you roughly the result of the questioning of fifty or more persons at random in the week — a praying remnant have been agonising before God about the state of the beloved land, and it is through that the answer of fire has come. You tell me that the revival originates with Roberts. I tell you that Roberts is a product of the revival. You tell me that it began in an Endeavour meeting where a dear girl bore testimony. I tell you that was part of the result of a revival breaking out everywhere. If you and I could stand above Wales, looking at it, you would see fire breaking out here, and there, and yonder, and somewhere else, without any collusion or pre-arrangement. It is a Divine visitation in which God — let me say this reverently — in which God is saying to us: See what I can do without the things you are depending on; see what I can do in answer to a praying people; see what I can do through the simplest, who are ready to fall in line, and depend wholly and absolutely upon me.

What is the character of this revival? It is a Church revival. I do not mean by that merely a revival among church members. It is that, but it is held in church buildings. Now, you may look astonished, but I have been saying for a long time that the revival which is to be permanent in the life of a nation must be associated with the life of the churches. What I am looking for is that there shall come a revival breaking out in all our regular church life. The meetings are held in the chapels, all up and down the valleys, and it began among church members, and when it touches the outside man it makes him into a church member at once. I am tremendous-

ly suspicious of any mission or revival movement that treats with
contempt the Church of Christ, and affects to despise the churches.
Within five weeks 20,000 have joined the churches.

20,000 HAVE JOINED THE CHURCHES

I think more than that have been converted, but the churches in
Wales have enrolled during the last five weeks 20,000 new members. It is a movement in the Church, and of the Church, a movement; in which the true functions and forces of the Church are being exercised and filled.

Now, what effect is this work producing upon men? First of all,
it is turning Christians everywhere into evangelists. There is nothing more remarkable about it than that, I think. People you never
expected to see doing this kind of thing are becoming definite personal workers. Let me give you an illustration. A friend of mine
went to one of the meetings, and he walked down to the meeting
with an old friend of his, a deacon of the Congregational Church, a
man whose piety no one doubted, a man who for long years had
worked in the life of the Church in some of its departments, but a
man who never would think of speaking to men about their souls,
although he would not have objected to someone else doing it. As
my friend walked down with the deacon, the deacon said to him, "I
have eighteen young men in an athletic class of which I am president. I hope some of them will be in the meeting to-night." There
was a new manifestation. Within fifteen minutes he left his seat by
my friend and was seen talking to a young man down in front of
him. Presently the deacon rose and said, "Thank God for So and
So," giving his name, "he has given his heart to Christ right here."
In a moment or two he left him, and was with another young man.
Before that meeting closed that deacon had led every one of those
eighteen young men to Jesus Christ, who never before thought of
speaking to men about their souls.

My own friend, with whom I stayed, who has always been reticent of speaking to men, told me how, sitting in his office, there
surged upon him the great conviction that he ought to go and speak

to another man with whom he had done business for long years. My friend suddenly put down his pen, and left his office, and went on 'Change, and there he saw the very man, and going up to him, passing the time of day to him, the man said to him, "What do you think of this Revival?" And my friend looked him squarely in the eye and said, "How is it with your own soul?" The man looked back at him, and said, "Last night at twelve, from some unknown reason, I had to get out of bed and give myself to Jesus Christ, and I was hungering for someone to come and talk to me." Here is a man turned into an evangelist by supernatural means. If this is emotional, then God send us more of it! Here is a cool, calculating business ship-owner, that I have known all my life, leaving his office to go on 'Change and ask a man about his soul.

Another characteristic is that you never know just where this fire is going to break out next. A preacher in one of the towns down there said, "I have got a sermon in my pocket. It has been there for three weeks. I went down to my church three Sundays ago with a sermon prepared, my notes in my pocket, and that morning some man broke out in testimony, and it was followed by prayer and singing, and it has never ceased, but two hundred people have joined the church." He said, "I am keeping that sermon!"

DOWN IN ONE OF THE MINES

The other day —and I hope you understand I am only repeating to you the instances that came under my personal observation— the other day in one of the mines, a collier was walking along, and he came, to his great surprise, to where one of the principal officials in the mine was standing. The official said, "Jim, I have been waiting two hours here for you." "Have you, sir?" said Jim. "What do you want?" "I want to be saved, Jim." The man said, "Let us get right down here," and there in the mine the colliery official, instructed by the collier, passed into the Kingdom of God. When he got up he said, "Tell all the men, tell everybody you meet, I am converted." Straightway confession.

The horses are terribly puzzled. A manager said to me, "The

haulers are some of the very lowest. They have driven their horses by obscenity and kicks. Now they can hardly persuade the horses to start working, because there is no obscenity and no kicks." The movement is characterised by the most remarkable confessions of sin, confessions that must be costly. I heard some of them, men rising who have been members of the church, and officers of the church, confessing hidden sin in their heart, impurity committed and condoned, and seeking prayer for its putting away. The whole movement is marvellously characterised by a confession of Jesus Christ, testimony to His power, to His goodness, to His beneficence, and testimony merging for evermore into outbursts of singing, New let us stand back a little further and speak of the essential notes, as I have noticed some of the incidental peculiarities.

THE ESSENTIAL NOTES

I say to you to-day, beloved, without any hesitation, that this whole thing is of God, that it is a visitation in which he is making men conscious of Himself, ,without any human agency. The Revival is far more widespread than the fire zone. In this sense you may understand that the fire zone is where the meetings are actually held, and where you feel the flame that burns, But even when you come out of it, and go into railway trains, or into a shop, a bank, anywhere, men everywhere are talking of God, Whether they obey or not is another matter. There are thousands who have not yielded to the constraint of God, but God has given Wales in these days a new conviction and consciousness of Himself. That is the profound thing, the underlying truth.

And then another essential note to be remembered is this. I have already said that it is essentially a Church Revival in the broadest sense of that word. What is the Church doing ? If you go to Wales and get near this work you will see the Church returning to the true functions of her priesthood. What are the functions of the Christian priesthood ? Of course I need hardly stay to say that I am referring to the priesthood of the Church, for there is no priesthood in the Church separated from the Church; and I am not at all sure that

God is not restoring to Wales the true functions of priesthood, partly because she refuses to be dominated by any false system of priesthood. There are two essential functions to the Christian priesthood: The first is eucharistic, the giving of thanks; the other is intercessory, praying. That is all. That is going on. The Church everywhere singing and praying and offering praise, and pleading with God. Every meeting is made up almost exclusively of these things. Evan Roberts, and those who sing with him, and those who are speaking in other parts, are urging the people to praise, to pray, and the Church everywhere is doing it; and while the Church is praising, singing plaintively in Welsh such songs as

> "Oh, the Lamb, the gentle Lamb,
> The Lamb of Calvary,"

or while the Church is singing of the love of God, men and women are coming down broken-hearted, sin-convicted, yielding themselves to Jesus Christ. It is a great return on the part of the Church, under the inspired touch of the Spirit of God, to the exercise of its priestly functions—giving praise and interceding.

And then it is a great recognition of the presence and power of the Spirit manifesting itself in the glorification of Christ. What are the effects produced upon the converts?

EFFECTS PRODUCED UPON THE CONVERTS?

Again I am taking the largest outlook. Two words, I think, cover the whole thing—vision and virtue. Men are seeing things! Oh, yes, it is quite cheap and easy to stay at a distance and smile. It is intensely easy for the Lancet to predict insanity. I will tell you something in passing. The insanity that will be produced in Wales by this Welsh Revival will be as nothing to the insanity from drink which it will cure.

It is intensely cheap and easy for cold-blooded men at a distance, who know nothing of Celtic fire or spiritual fire, to smile at this whole thing, this seeing of visions. But while you smile, these

men are seeing visions. They will tell you crudely of them, perhaps, but it is one of those strange things that no man can ever tell
of a vision when he sees it really. They are seeing God. Well, but
you say that will pass. It is passing. The vision is passing out into
virtue, and men are paying their debts, and abandoning the public-
house, and treating their horses well. Oh, my masters! Did you say
the next Revival would be ethical? It is that, because it is spiritual,
and you will never get an ethical revival except in this way. Vision
is merging into virtue, and theatrical companies are packing up and
going back because there are no houses, and on every hand there is
sweeping down these Welsh valleys a great clean river. It is the river of God, and men are being cleansed in it, in personal and civic
relationships. We are quite willing to appeal to the coming years
about this work, but the evidences are already present on every
hand. Tradesmen are being startled by men paying debts even
though the statute of limitations has run out. Tradesmen, you know
what that means! An emotion that will make a man do that is worth
cultivating, and it is good all the way through.

This is very fragmentary, but it must be if a man talks of these
things. No man ever yet could describe a burning bush, and I know
I have not described this to you.

Will you let me hold you while I say something to you about
OUR OWN LESSONS?

First of all as to Wales itself, and especially to this great district.
I am perfectly sure that it will be a good thing for us if we let it
alone. By that I mean that General Booth never manifested his wisdom more than when he packed up and came home. And I love
him, and have for years. Any of us that go down there with any
thought in our heart we can help, we had better leave the thing in
God's hand. To me it is so sacred a manifestation and glorious that
I became frightened, as it wore on, lest my presence, without any
desire that it should be so, should check the great movement. That
was why I said to Evan Roberts, "I am going away, man, because I
will not, so help me God, hinder by five minutes this great work." I
feel we had better let that thing run. We did not originate it any-

where, and— forgive the Americanism—we cannot run it. We had better stand aside and pray, and get ready for what God means to do for us.

What are the great values of this movement in Wales?

THE GREAT VALUES OF THIS MOVEMENT

First, the reaffirmation of the spiritual. Secondly, this marvellous union of the spiritual with the practical, this manifestation of an ethical result from a spiritual renewal. Let me say it. I am not at all sure that God is not rebuking our over-organization. We certainly have been in danger of thinking there could not be a Revival, or any work done for God, unless we had prepared everywhere. I am the last man to speak against organization in its proper place, but I am inclined to think God is saying to us, Your organizations are right providing you do not live in them, and end in them. But here, apart from all of them, setting them almost ruthlessly on one side, Pentecostal power and fire are being manifested.

What shall we do in the presence of this great movement? Imitate it? Imitation will be fatal. Let no man come back and attempt to start anywhere in London meetings on the lines of those held In Wales, and for this simple reason: that no man started them there. If somewhere here there should break out some great manifestation such as this, then God grant we be ready to fall in line. You cannot imitate this kind of thing. What shall we do? If we cannot imitate, we can discover the principles. What are they? Let us listen for the Spirit, confess Christ, be absolutely at His disposal. Oh, but you say to me, Are not we all that? Well, I do not know. God help us to find out for ourselves. I think we are in terrible danger of listening to the Spirit, and when His voice speaks to us, quenching Him. You say, Something moved me to speak to that man about his soul, but I did not like to. That is how Revival is stopped. Speak to him. Listening to the Spirit, confessing Christ openly; absolutely at His disposal.

Let us in our Church work, not attempt to imitate the thing afar, but let us prayerfully take hold of every organization and every method, and strengthen it. Strengthen it how? By seeing to it that through the organization the Spirit of God has right of way; by bringing your Sunday-school class, dear teacher, into a new realm, and instead of treating it as a company of boys and girls you care for very much, that you teach and interest on Sunday afternoons, treat it as a company of souls to be saved. Begin to try and teach along that line; instead of treating our congregations as congregations to be instructed ever in holy things, treat them as men and women that are to be persuaded to holy things, and consecration, and Jesus Christ. And in order to the doing of all this, what we supremely need is that we ourselves should be at the end of ourselves, that we should dare to abandon ourselves with some amount of passion to our work. Oh, we have been too

> "Icily regular, faultily faultless,
> Splendidly null."

What we do need is the abandonment of ourselves to the great truths we know so well, to the great forces that indwell. Let us "strengthen the things that remain."

And so—now forgive me if I address myself to my own people—shall we not turn ourselves—ministers and staff and officers, and all the members, and shall we not say, at least we can now take up this work and make it instinct with new devotion and life, at least we can take hold of the thing that lies closest, and put into it the passion of a great devotion. We can begin there. The Church of God needs three things.

CHURCH OF GOD NEEDS THREE THINGS

It needs first to set itself to get things out of the way for God. I appreciate the almost puzzled look upon some of your faces. What things? I do not know. All the things that are in His way: Your habit that you know is unholy; your method of business that will not bear the light of day; your unforgiving heart towards a Church member. Oh, God forgive me that I mention anything! You know, you know. They are in God's way, these things. They must be cleared out. That is the first thing. There may be other things in God's way. Any organization in Church life that does not make for the salvation of men is a fungus growth, and the sooner we drop it off the better. Oh, I know churches where classrooms are so tremendously full there is no room for a prayer meeting. Are we ready to put things out of the way for God? I think we are. I think that if God manifests Himself, and men begin to be saved, I do not think there is a Guild Social we will keep. I do not think there is any bazaar coming on that will hinder it! Oh, if there is anything, we must be prepared to sweep everything out for God to have highway. That is the attitude the Church must be prepared to take. Now let me say also to the other Churches, that is the true attitude.

THE TRUE ATTITUDE

There is nothing so important as the saving of men, and when the Church says that, and is ready, God will come. We need then to wait upon Him in earnest, constant prayer. Oh, brothers, sisters, pray, pray alone; pray in secret; pray together; and pray out of a sense of London's sin and sorrow. It is so easy to be familiar with these things, until they have lost their power to touch us. Oh, the sin and the sorrow of London! May God lay it upon our hearts as a burden. And out of that agony let us begin to pray, and go forward the moment He opens the door, and indicates the way. I do not expect—and especially to young Christians do I say this—I do not expect just the same kind of manifestation. God always manifests Himself through the natural temperament, and you can never have the poetic fire and fervour of a Celtic Revival in London. But you can have a stern, hard, magnificent consecration, and results that characterize your own nationality. Are we ready for God? I feel like apologizing to you tonight for this broken talk. I have talked out of my heart. I have tried to talk of fire that cannot be described. I have tried to talk out of the tremendous sense that God is abroad, and I talk out of the desire that I cannot express—that somewhere, somewhen, somehow, He may put out His hand, and shake this city for the salvation of men.

4: Mr. Evan Roberts
By W. T. STEAD
(Editor of the British 'Review of Reviews')

MR. EVAN ROBERTS is the central figure, so far as there is any central figure, of the religious awakening in Wales. The Revival is not like the Moody and Sankey awakening, or the Torrey and Alexander Mission, or the organised Revivalism of the Salvation Army, of any one man or one organization. Never in the history of Revivals has there been any Revival more spontaneous than this. It has burst out here, there, and everywhere, without leaders, or organization, or direction. Hence, if Mr. Evan Roberts is spoken of as the centre, it is only because it happens to be one of the few conspicuous figures in a movement which he neither organised nor controls.

I attended three meetings at Mardy in the Rhondda Valley on Sunday, sat beside him on the platform, and had tea with him at a friend's house. After tea Mr. Roberts consented to an interview. He was simple and unaffected; absolutely free from any vanity or spiritual pride. He spoke in English with considerable ease, but his hearers say that it is only when he uses his Welsh tongue that they hear the melody of his voice.

"The movement is not of me," said Mr. Roberts— "it is of God. I would not dare to try to direct it. Obey the Spirit, that is our word in everything. It is the Spirit alone which is leading us in our meetings and in all that is done."

"You do not preach, or teach, or control the meetings?"

"Why should I teach when the Spirit is teaching? What need

have these people to be told that they are sinners? What they need is salvation. Do they not know it? It is not knowledge that they lack, but decision—action. And why should I control the meetings? The meetings control themselves, or rather the Spirit that is in them controls them."

"You find the ministry of the Singing Sisters useful?"

"Most useful. They go with me wherever I go. I never part from them without feeling that something is absent if they are not there. The singing is very important, but not everything. No. The public confession is also important—more so than the speaking. True, I talk to them a little. But the meetings go of themselves."

"Do you propose to go to England?"

"No. To North Wales next. They say North Wales is stony cold, but I believe the Holy Spirit will work there also. Oh, yes, God will move North Wales also."

"Can you tell me how you began to take to this work?"

"Oh, yes, that I will," said Mr. Roberts, "if you wish to hear of it. For a long, long time I was much troubled in my soul and my heart by thinking over the failure of Christianity. Oh! it seemed such a failure—such a failure—and I prayed and prayed, but nothing seemed to give me any relief. But one night, after I had been in great distress praying about this, I went to sleep, and at one o'clock in the morning suddenly I was waked up out of my sleep, and I found myself with unspeakable joy and awe in the very presence of the Almighty God. And for the space of four hours I was privileged to speak face to face with Him as a man speaks face to face with a friend. At five o'clock it seemed to me as if I again returned to earth."

"Were you not dreaming?" I asked.

"No, I was wide awake. And it was not only that morning, but every morning for three or four months. Always I enjoyed four hours of that wonderful communion with God. I cannot describe it. I felt it, and it seemed to change all my nature, and I saw things in a different light, and I knew that God was going to work in the land, and not this land only, but in all the world."

"Excuse me," I said, "but, as an old interviewer, may I ask if, when the mystic ecstasy passed, you put on paper all that you remembered of these times of communion?"

"No, I write nothing at all," said Mr. Roberts. "It went on all the time until I had to go to Newcastle Emlyn to the college to prepare for the ministry. I dreaded to go for fear I should lose these four hours with God every morning. But I had to go, and it happened as I feared. For a whole month He came no more, and I was in darkness. And my heart became as a stone. Even the sight of the Cross brought no tears to my eyes. So it continued until, to my great joy, He returned to me, and I had again the glorious communion. And He said I must go and speak to my people in my own village. But I did not go. I did not feel as if I could go to speak to my own people."

May I ask," I said, "if He of whom you speak appeared to you as Jesus Christ?"

"No," said Mr. Roberts, "not so; it was the personal God, not as Jesus."

"As God the Father Almighty?" I said.

"Yes," said Mr. Roberts, "and the Holy Spirit."

"Pardon me," I said, "but I interrupted you. Pray go on."

"I did not go to my people, but I was troubled and ill at ease. And one Sunday, as I sat in the chapel, I could not fix my mind upon the service, for always before my eyes I saw, as in a vision, the schoolroom in Lougher, where I live. And there, sitting in rows before me, I saw my old companions and all the young people, and I saw myself addressing them. I shook my head impatiently, and strove to drive away this vision, but it always came back. And I heard a voice in my inward ear as plain as anything saying, 'Go and speak to these people.' And for a long time I would not. But the pressure became greater and greater, and I could hear nothing of the sermon. Then at last I could resist no longer, and I said, 'Well, Lord, if it is Thy will, I will go.' Then instantly the vision vanished, and the whole chapel became filled with light so dazzling that I could faintly see the minister in the pulpit, and between him and me the glory as of the light of the sun in Heaven."

"And then you went home?"

"No; I went to my tutor and told him all things, and asked him if he believed that it was of God or of the devil? And he said the devil does not put good thoughts into the mind. I must go and obey the heavenly vision. So I went back to Lougher, and I saw my own minister, and him also I told. And he said that I might try and see what I could do, but that the ground was stony and the task would be hard."

"Did you find it so?"

"I asked the young people to come together, for I wanted to talk to them. They came and I stood up to talk to them,' and, behold, it was even as I had seen in the church at Newcastle Emlyn. The young people sat as I had seen them sitting all together in rows before me, and I was speaking to them even as it had been shown to me. At first they did not seem inclined to listen; but I went on, and at last the power of the Spirit came down and six came out for Jesus. But I was not satisfied. Oh, Lord,' I said, 'give me six more—I must have six more!' And we prayed together. At last the seventh came, and then the eighth and the ninth together, and after a time the tenth, and then the eleventh, and last of all came the twelfth also. But no more. And they saw that the Lord had given me the second six, and they began to believe in the power of prayer."

"Then after that you went on?"

"First I tried to speak to some other young people in another church, and asked them to come. But the news had gone out, and the old people said, 'May we not come too?' And I could not refuse them. So they came, and they kept on coming. Now here, now there all the time, and I have never had time to go back to college."

Not much chance, indeed, at present. Three meetings every day, lasting, with breaks for meals, from ten A. M. till twelve P. M., and sometimes later, leave scant leisure for studying elsewhere than in the hearts and souls of men. If only his body will hold out and his nervous system not give way, he will have time to study hereafter. At present he has other work in hand.

5. The Story Of The Awakening
As Seen By W. T. STEAD

THE Revival in Wales began in Cardiganshire. For a long time past the Welsh Christians had been moved to pray specially for the quickening of religious life in their midst. The impulse appears to have been sporadic and spontaneous. In remote country hamlets, in mining villages buried in distant valleys, one man or one woman would have it laid upon his or her soul to pray that the Holy Spirit might be poured out upon the cause in which they were spiritually concerned. There does not seem to have been any organized effort anywhere. It was all individual, local, and strictly limited to the neighborhood. An old Salvationist, for instance, suddenly had it borne in upon him that he was nearing the point from which no traveler returns. Of his own future he had no doubt. But what of the future of the others whom he so soon must leave, and leave forever?

Spiritual life was languishing in his local corps. No one was being converted. So he determined to give himself to prayer and fasting, giving Heaven no peace or rest all day or all night until the blessing came. One whole day he fasted, and the whole of the following night he prayed. And lo! it seemed as if the windows of Heaven were opened and showers of blessing descended upon the dry parched ground. The Revival broke out in his corps and many souls were gathered in. A similar blessing was enjoyed by one of the churches in the village, but it passed over the rest. Some, like Gideon's fleece, were drenched with dew, while all around the land was dry.

The story of the very first outbreak of the Revival traces it to the trembling utterance of a poor Welsh girl, who, at a meeting in a Cardigan village, was the first to rise and testify. "If no one else will, then I must say that I love the Lord Jesus Christ with all my heart." The pathos and the passion of the avowal acted like an electric shock upon the congregation. One after another rose and made the full surrender, and the news spread like wildfire from place to place that the Revival had broken out, and that souls were being ingathered to the Lord. But the Revival was soon to find its focus in a young theological student of the name of Evan Roberts, who had abandoned his course at Newcastle Emlyn to carry on the work of the Revival throughout Wales. His own simple story of how he came to the work is told elsewhere in this booklet.

I went down to South Wales to see for myself what was going on. I described my impressions in the Daily Chronicle, the Christian World, and the Methodist Times. I cannot do better than reproduce my report:

"The British Empire," as Admiral Fisher is never tired of repeating, "floats upon the British Navy." But the British Navy steams on Welsh coal. The driving force of all our battleships is hewn from the mines of these Welsh valleys, by the men among whom this remarkable religious awakening has taken place. This morning, as the slow train crawled down the gloomy valleys—for there was the mirk of coming snow in the air, and there was no sun in the sky—I could not avoid the obvious and insistent suggestion of the thought that Welsh religious enthusiasm may be destined to impart as compelling an impulse to the churches of the world as Welsh coal supplies to its navies.

Nor was the force of the suggestion weakened when, after attending three prolonged services at Mardy, a village of 5,000 inhabitants lying on the other side of Pontypridd, I found the flame of Welsh religious enthusiasm as smokeless as its coal. There are no advertisements, no brass bands, no posters, no huge tents. All the paraphernalia of the got-up job are conspicuous by their absence.

Neither is there any organization, nor is there a director, at least none that is visible to human eye. In the crowded chapels they even dispense with instrumental music. On Sunday night no note issued from the organ pipes. There was no need of instruments, for in and around and above and beneath surged the all-pervading thrill and throb of a multitude praying, and singing as they prayed.

The vast congregations were as soberly sane, as orderly, and at least as reverent as any congregation I ever saw beneath the dome of St. Paul's, when I used to go to hear Canon Liddon, the Chrysostom of the English pulpit. But it was aflame with a passionate religious enthusiasm, the like of which I have never seen in St. Paul's. Tier above tier from the crowded aisles to the loftiest gallery sat or stood, as necessity dictated, eager hundreds of serious men and thoughtful women, their eyes riveted upon the platform or upon whatever other part of the building was the storm centre of the meeting.

There was absolutely nothing wild, violent, hysterical, unless it be hysterical for the labouring breast to heave with sobbing that cannot be repressed, and the throat to choke with emotion as a sense of the awful horror and shame of a wasted life suddenly bursts upon the soul. On all sides there was the solemn gladness of men and women upon whose eyes has dawned the splendour of a new day, the foretaste of whose glories they are enjoying in the quickened sense of human fellowship and a keen glad zest added to their own lives.

The most thorough-going materialist who resolutely and forever rejects as inconceivable the existence of the soul in man, and to whom "the universe is but the infinite empty eye-socket of a dead God," could not fail to be impressed by the pathetic sincerity of these men; nor, if he were just, could he refuse to recognise that out of their faith in the creed which he has rejected, they have drawn and are drawing a motive power that makes for righteousness, and not only for righteousness, but for the joy of living, that he would be powerless to give them.

Employers tell me that the quality of the work the miners are putting in has improved. Waste is less, men go to their daily toil with a new spirit of gladness in their labour. In the long, dim galleries of the mine, where once the haulers swore at their ponies in Welshified English terms of blasphemy, there is now but to be heard the haunting melody of the revival music. The pit ponies, like the American mules, having been driven by oaths and curses since they first bore the yoke, are being re-trained to do their work without the incentive of profanity.

There is less drinking, less idleness, less gambling. Men record with almost incredulous amazement, how one football player after another has foresworn cards and drink and the gladiatorial games, and is living a sober and godly life, putting his energy into the revival. More wonderful still, and almost incredible to those who know how journalism lives and thrives upon gambling, is the fact that the most conservative daily paper of South Wales has devoted its columns day after day to reporting and defending the movement which declares war to the death against both gambling and drink.

How came this strange uplift of the earnestness of a whole community? Who can say? The wind bloweth where it listeth. Some tell you one thing, some another. All agree that it began some few months ago in Cardiganshire, eddied hither and thither, spreading like fire from valley to valley, until, as one observer said to me, "Wherever it came from, or however it began, all South Wales to-day is in a flame."

However it began. So it is going on. "If no one else, then I must." It is "Here am I, send me!" This public self-consecration, this definite and decisive avowal of a determination to put under their feet their dead past of vice and sin and indifference, and to reach out towards a higher ideal of human existence, is going on everywhere in South Wales. Nor, if we think of it sanely and look at it in the right perspective, is there a nobler spectacle appealing more directly to the highest instincts of our nature to be seen in all the world to-day.

At Mardy, where I spent Sunday, the miners are voluntarily taxing themselves to build an institute, public hall, library, and reading -room. By their express request the money is deducted from their

wages on payday. They have created a library of 2,000 books, capitally selected and well used. They have about half a dozen chapels
and churches, a co-operative society, and the usual appliances of
civilization. They have every outward and visible sign of industrial
prosperity. It is a mining village pure and simple, industrial democracy in its nakedest primitive form.

In this village I attended three meetings on Sunday— two and a
half hours in the morning, two and a half hours in the afternoon,
and two hours at night, when I had to leave to catch the train. At all
these meetings the same kind of thing went on, the same kind of
congregations assembled, the same strained, intense emotion was
manifest. Aisles were crowded. Pulpit stairs were packed, and,
'mirabile dictu!' two-thirds of the congregation were men and at
least one-half young men.

"There," said one, "is the hope and the glory of the movement."
Here and there is a grey head. But the majority of the congregation
were stalwart young miners, who gave the meeting all the fervour
and swing and enthusiasm of youth. The revival had been going on
in Mardy for a fortnight. All the churches had been holding services every night with great results. At the Baptist Church they had
to report the addition of nearly fifty members, fifty were waiting
for baptism, thirty—five backsliders had been reclaimed.

In Mardy the fortnight's services had resulted in 500 conversions. And this, be it noted, when each place of worship was going
"on its own." Mr. Evan Roberts, the so-called boy preacher of the
revival, and his singing sisterhood, did not reach Mardy until the
Sunday of my visit.

I have called Evan Roberts the so-called boy preacher, because
he is neither a boy nor a preacher. He is a tall, graceful, good-
looking young man of twenty-six, with a pleading eye and a most
winsome smile. If he is a boy, he is a six-foot boy, and six-footers
are usually past their boyhood. As he is not a boy, neither is he a
preacher. He talks simply, unaffectedly, earnestly now and then,
but he makes no sermons, and preaching is emphatically not the
note of this Revival in the west. If it has been by the foolishness of

preaching that men have been saved heretofore, that agency seems as if it were destined to take a back seat in the present movement.

The revival is borne along upon billowing waves of sacred song. It is the singing, not the preaching, that is the instrument which is most efficacious in striking the hearts of men. In this respect these services in the Welsh chapel reminded me strangely of the beautiful liturgical services of the Greek church, notably in St. Isaac's, of St. Petersburg, on Easter morn, and in the receptions of the pilgrims at the Troitski monastery, near Moscow.

The most extraordinary thing about the meetings which I attended was the extent to which they were absolutely without any human direction or leadership. "We must obey the Spirit," is the watchword of Evan Roberts, and he is as obedient as the humblest of his followers. The meetings open—after any amount of preliminary singing while the congregation is assembling—by the reading of a chapter or a psalm. Then it is go as you please for two hours or more.

And the amazing thing is that it does go and does not get entangled in what might seem to be inevitable confusion. Three-fourths of the meeting consists of singing. No one uses a hymnbook. No one gives out a hymn. The last person to control the meeting in any way is Mr. Evan Roberts. People pray and sing, give testimony or exhort as the Spirit moves them. As a study of the psychology of crowds I have seen nothing like it. You feel that the thousand or fifteen hundred persons before you have become merged into one myriad-headed, but single-souled personality.

You can watch what they call the influence of the power of the Spirit playing over the crowded congregation as an eddying wind plays over the surface of a pond. If anyone carried away by his feelings prays too long, or if anyone when speaking fails to touch the right note, someone—it may be anybody—commences to sing. For a moment there is a hesitation as if the meeting were in doubt as to its decision, whether to hear the speaker or to continue to join in the prayer, or whether to sing. If it decides to hear and to pray the singing dies away. If, on the other hand, as usually happens, the people decide to sing, the chorus swells in volume until it drowns all other sound.

A very remarkable instance of this abandonment of the meeting to the spontaneous impulse, not merely of those within the walls, but of those crowded outside, who were unable to get in, occurred on Sunday night. Twice the order of proceeding, if order it can be called, was altered by the crowd outside, who, being moved by some mysterious impulse, started a hymn on their own account, which was at once taken up by the congregation within. On one of these occasions Evan Roberts was addressing the meeting. He at once gave way, and the singing became general.

The prayers are largely autobiographical, and some of them intensely dramatic. On one occasion an impassioned and moving appeal to the Deity was accompanied throughout by an exquisitely rendered hymn, sung by three of the Singing Sisters. It was like the undertone of the orchestra when some leading singer is holding the house.

The Singing Sisters—there are five of them, one, Mme. Morgan, who was a professional singer—are as conspicuous figures in the movement as Evan Roberts himself. Some of their solos are wonders of dramatic and musical appeal. Nor is the effect lessened by the fact that the singers, like the speakers, sometimes break down in sobs and tears. The meeting always breaks out into a passionate and consoling song, until the soloist having recovered her breath, rises from her knees and resumes her song.

The praying and singing are both wonderful, but more impressive than either are the breaks which occur when utterance can no more, and the sobbing in the silence, momentarily heard, is drowned in a tempest of melody. No need for an organ. The assembly was its own organ as a thousand sorrowing or rejoicing hearts found expression in the sacred psalmody of their native hills.

Repentance, open confession, intercessory prayer, and, above all else, this marvelous musical liturgy—a liturgy unwritten but heartfelt, a mighty chorus rising like the thunder of the surge on a rock-bound shore, ever and anon broken by the flutelike note of the Singing Sisters, whose melody was as sweet and as spontaneous as the music of the throstle in the grove or the lark in the sky. And all this vast quivering, throbbing, singing, praying, exultant multitude intensely conscious of the all-pervading influence of some invisible reality—now for the first time moving palpable though not tangible in their midst.

They called it the Spirit of God. Those who have not witnessed it may call it what they will; I am inclined to agree with those on the spot. For man, being according to the orthodox, evil, can do no good thing of himself, so, as Cardinal Manning used to say, "Wherever you behold a good thing, there you see the working of the Holy Ghost." And the revival, as I saw it, was emphatically a good thing.

6: The Psychology of The Revival
By W. T. Stead

Revivalism is much decried among the superior per sons who pride themselves upon their freedom from superstition, their detachment from the vulgarity of popular religion, their philosophic aloofness from the great emotions, the noble aspirations and the fiery enthusiasms of humanity. The purblind eunuchs! without vision or virility, what matters it what they say? Mr.

Gladstone once defined radicalism as liberalism in earnest. Revivalism may be denned as Christianity in earnest -- impatiently in earnest to produce an immediate impression on the heart and consciousness of men.

Revivalism differs from the ordinary conventional methods of religious teaching in that it concentrates all its efforts upon the supreme point of inducing individuals to take, there and then, the fateful decision upon which their whole future depends. To rouse men from apathy and indifference, to compel them to face squarely the eternal alternative, to leave them no subterfuge or evasion, to bring to bear upon hesitating and doubting souls the pressure necessary to induce a definite acceptance of the service of Christ -- this is revivalism. In one form or another it has always flourished, and will always flourish wherever there is a great difference of moral temperature among men. Mr. Gladstone in Mid lothian affords a supreme type of the successful revivalist in politics. Peter the Hermit was a revivalist of another type. But for the most part revivalism means a spiritual awakening, the conversion of individuals who, from living in indifference or in vice, turn from their evil ways and lead new lives in which, however imperfectly, they endeavour consciously to follow Christ.

So far from revivalism being opposed to the teaching of modern science, it is nothing more or less than the practical application to the human heart of principles set forth by the latest psychological science. Professor William James's book on "The Varieties of Religious Experience" contains two chapters on "Conversion" which should be attentively studied by all who are anxious to understand the rationale of revivalism, the psychological law which is seen in operation in conversion. According to Professor James, the unconverted man is like a capsized boat which is floating bottom upwards on the sea of life. All the beneficent influences and ethical agencies which collectively are lumped together by religious folk as the grace of God, are ceaselessly employed in endeavoring to shift the center of gravity, so as to enable the boat to right herself. They operate in many ways— sometimes by pumping out the water, at other times by forcing in air; but always their aim and object is to so change her equilibrium as to enable her to get upon her keel again.

Professor James points out that in the subliminal mind, in the human soul that lies beneath the active consciousness, in the vast region in which are stored all the latent memories and the automatic instincts of the mind, there may be going on, during periods in which the man is apparently utterly indifferent to anything but sensual indulgence, a process analogous to that in which, even in the depths of winter, the plants are preparing for the leaves and flowers of spring. Or to return to the original metaphor— which is my own, although suggested by Professor James's lectures— the capsized ship while floating bottom upwards may all the while be experiencing a steady increase in her buoyancy caused by the pumping in of air and the consequent expulsion of water. This process, invisible to the observer, will at a given moment achieve such results that a mere push from the outside will cause the ship to right herself, because the conditions of equilibrium have been supplied, and all that was needed was an impetus from without. Just so it is with the unconverted man in times of revival.

The revivalist or the contagious emotion of a great popular enthusiasm administers the thrust that alone is needed to secure the outward and visible manifestation of the long preceding growth of the grace of God in the soul. Who can tell how many millions there are in the land at the present time who are only waiting the push that revivalism gives, as in windy March the crocuses but wait a gleam of sunshine to put forth their blossoms? The instantaneous nature of the conversions effected in revivals merely shows that souls, like ships, are capable of righting themselves in a moment, when the proper conditions of a stable right-side-up equilibrium have been achieved. It is an awe-inspiring thought that there may be millions of our English folk who are at this moment in a condition of such unstable equilibrium that a word, a touch, may turn them over. They are ready for conversion. Their subliminal self all unconsciously is charged with the Divine Spirit which at the slightest outer impact may astonish everyone, themselves most of all, by presenting to the world what the theologians call "a new creature in Christ Jesus." But although that new creature may be born in a day, he was conceived long ago, and the gestation of the soul of a Christian often lasts more years than his body took months.

However we may explain it, the very skeptical must admit that what the revivalist seeks to effect is of all things the most important object of human endeavor. No political or social change can be regarded as having any serious importance, excepting so far as it tends to facilitate indirectly the achievement of the same result which the revivalist seeks directly. The aim of all reformers is the regeneration of the individual. To make a bad man good, a cruel man merciful, a lazy man industrious, a drunkard sober, and to substitute selfless struggle to help others for a selfish scramble to seize everything for oneself— that is the aim-all, the be-all and the end-all of all those who seek the improvement of society and the progress of the world. It makes no difference whether the reformer is called Blatchford or Liddon, Bradlaugh or Price Hughes, John Morley or General Booth, Frederic Harrison or the Archbishop of

Canterbury, the President of the Free Thinkers' Congress or the Pope of Rome— that is what they are all after— that, and in the ultimate, nothing but that. And when it comes to be looked at scientifically, there is none of the whole diversified multitude of social, religious and political reformers who can deny that a great religious revival does succeed in achieving the results which they desire more rapidly, more decisively, and in a greater number of cases than any other agency known to mankind. We may discount it as much as we like. But the facts are there. It is not necessary to credit the revival with all the results which it reveals, any more than we may credit a day's sunshine in spring with all the flowers it brings to birth. But it brings them out. So does a revival. And if there had been no revival, the latent sainthood of multitudes would never have been born, just as the flowers would never come out in May if there were no sun.

It is often argued that revivalism is ephemeral. So are apple blossoms. But apples are born of them. And as the brief historical retrospect shows, the fruits of revivals are among the most permanent things in history. People who sneer at the backsliders after a revival forget that it is a good thing for a man to have quit drinking, and dog-fighting, and wife-beating for a week or a month, even if after that period during which he struggled to live a human life he returns like a sow to wallowing in the mire. But, as a matter of fact, while some undoubtedly fall away, and very few indeed ever permanently retain the ecstasy and the vision of the moment of their conversion, the majority of converts made in times of revival remain steadfast.

There were, no doubt, a good many who fell away among the thousands added to the early Christian Church after the Day of Pentecost, but those who remained formed the Church which turned the world into Christendom. Professor Starbuck, who, in his "Psychology of Religion," made a minute analysis of one hundred cases of conversion, reports that while 93 percent of the women and 77 percent of the men bewailed their own backsliding, he found on examination that only 6 percent had really relapsed; the

backsliding of the others was only a change in the ardor of sentiment. His conclusion is notable. Conversion, he says, brings with it
a changed attitude towards life which is fairly constant and permanent, although the feelings fluctuate. In other words, the persons
who have passed through conversion, having once taken a stand for
the religious life, tend to feel themselves identified with it, no matter how much their religious enthusiasm declines.

7: The Teaching of the Revival
By Evan H Hopkins

It is important that, as intelligent Christians, we should seek to know the meaning of God's working, in the wonderful religious awakening now going on in Wales. We may be occupied too exclusively with the mere incidents of the movement— deeply impressive, thrilling, and important as they are. We may be taken up with the effects, without sufficiently recognizing the cause. Again, we may have our attention concentrated on what are the mere accidents of the movement— the noise, excitement, and intense emotionalism manifested at the meetings; and we may be led to suppose that if only all these phenomena can be reproduced in other places, the same blessed results will follow that are being realized in Wales. We may be tempted to imitate what are only the mere accidents of a real and divine working in the hearts of the people. All such attempts must end in failure, producing a reaction of unbelief in the imitators, and bringing dishonor on God's gracious awakening. May we be kept from all human efforts to "get up a revival."

Let us endeavored to learn what God is teaching us in this movement. If we are taught of Him He will show us the meaning of His working. He will enable us to distinguish between that which is merely accidental and that which is essential. We shall be enabled to look beneath the surface of this Divine visitation.

This revival is in some respects unlike those that have preceded it. God is showing us today what He can do, not so much through the individual missioner as through the whole company of believing people assembled together in His name. We have been accustomed to the Holy Spirit working through the pastor, or evangelist, directly upon the unconverted. But what we are witnessing today is the same Divine power working through the Church in its corporate capacity on those who are unsaved.

It is deeply instructive to see how God is using Evan Roberts in this movement. Crowds come from long distances to learn the secret of the wonderful power manifested at his meetings. They come often expecting to hear powerful addresses. Many have been surprised and disappointed to find that the evangelist has often remained silent for long intervals. But he has been occupied with something far more important than interesting them with an address. His soul has been concerned with the spiritual condition of the believers present, in their relation to God. Get the Church right with God, and then He will work through the Church on the unsaved. "Bend the Church, and save the world," is the watchword of this revival.

There are two things that impress one in Evan Roberts— the grace of self-effacement and the gift of spiritual discernment.

He will not gratify the spirit of curiosity. He will not receive honor from men. He knows that his place is in the background. His one desire in the meetings is to lead God's children into a condition of soul-harmony with Him. This thought seems to be deeply embedded in his being, that is: Let believers be as one before God in unity of life and love— in oneness of purpose and desire— and then the Holy Ghost, who is present, will put forth His power; God's children will be filled with the Spirit, and the unconverted will be saved.

Very solemn and searching are the words he addresses to the Christians present. It is to them, and not to the unsaved, that his words are chiefly directed. The effect is a brokenness of heart, a tenderness of spirit. But until the hindrances that may be in the hearts of God's children present are removed the power is lacking in the meeting. To this servant of God the gift of spiritual discernment seems to have been given in such a way that he is used chiefly in bringing God's children, by means of heart-searching confession and full consecration, into that spiritual condition in which the Holy Ghost can work with unhindered sway. It is through the Church that the Holy Ghost is working amongst the unconverted in this revival.

Oh, for this grace of self-effacement in all who have been called to occupy prominent positions in Christian work! How very few there are who are willing to be passed over, or lost sight of by the crowd! How much there is of self-advertisement even amongst the best of us. Let all so-called "leaders" in Christian work get down in the dust before God, and be ready, not only to say of themselves that they are empty, and helpless, and nothing, but be willing to accept that verdict when the same is said of them by others.

It is to the man who has the grace of self-effacement that God can add the gift of spiritual discernment. It is only such a one who is really equipped for the special work to which Evan Roberts has been called. Let us not cease to pray for him, that he may be kept thus humble and dependent upon God. He is at this time especially exposed to the danger that comes from well-meaning, but ill advised, Christians, who would tempt him to leave the work in which he is engaged to take the lead in some great campaign.

8: Experience of A Visitor From London

BEING assured, the morning after our arrival in Swansea, that in order to obtain a seat for the 2 P. M. meeting we must not be later than 11:30 at Ebenezer Chapel, we arrived at that hour, and found the place fast filling. In a few minutes an earnest English prayer from someone in the gallery started the meeting, which went on without a break for five and a half hours. The great preponderance of men, which had struck us on our former visit in the Rhondda Valley, was not so conspicuous here. There were a large number of women, and of children, too, and the markedly Welsh faces were interspersed with English residents and visitors.

But the same power from above was working. Prayer which was not for the ear of man, but of God, singing which was unto the Lord, testimony which the bursting gladness of a new life impelled, were the same here as in Ferndale.

Two distinguished clergymen of the Church of England— the Rev. and Hon. Talbot Rice, Vicar of Swansea, and the Rev. Barnes Lawrence, Vicar of Blackheath, one of the Keswick Committee— sat with several "Nonconformists" in the "big pew." But these well-known teachers took no prominent part in the proceedings; man was at a discount, and all were there to deal with God. "Where the Spirit of the Lord is, there is Liberty" (2 Cor. 3: 17) was fully exemplified in the gathering; men, women, English. Welsh, prayed or sang as they believed they were led of the Spirit. One was reminded of some of the more deeply spiritual meetings of the Society of Friends. Mr. Evan Roberts possesses, by God's grace, a remarkable spiritual discernment. Recently, on entering a meeting, he said:

"You are singing, but you are not worshipping; this is not singing unto the Lord." How one thought of the choirs in so many churches in which the singing always gives the impression that it is directed to the ears of the audience, not to the ear of God! There is in this revival a deep current of reality; when anything unreal creeps in, the power stops.

There was an earnest lad of sixteen years who came up into the "big pew," Bible in hand, but no break occurred for some time; he stood silent with a rapt expression, and when he read a portion in Welsh he just slipped away— he had obeyed the Spirit.

The following morning we started early to attend the services at Abertillery, a Monmouthshire colliery town, where 1,000 souls were reported as having found the Lord during the past few weeks; the whole population of the place is 15,000. Here Mr. Sidney Evans was expected. We needed no such efforts to secure seats as at Swansea. The meeting began just as elsewhere, by some full heart running over, and we were struck by the great spirit of prayer in this place. Being in English, we could join intelligently as well as spiritually.

There was an intense consciousness of the presence of God, and though some turned to look at the two very young men, Mr. Sidney Evans and his singing friend Mr. Samuel Jenkins, yet it was some little time before the prayer and singing ceased for them to take part.

Mr. Evans can hardly be more than eighteen; he has a pure, earnest, happy face, not so intense as his friend Mr. Evan Roberts. He said of himself, " Don't look to me for anything; I have nothing to give you; look to Jesus." He made some simple but striking remarks, and was most anxious that the whole company should look off unto Jesus.

The singing of Mr. Sam Jenkins was unique. With a face like a seraph, lit up from above, it was easy to see that he was occupied not with setting off his very fine voice, but in conveying a from his message Lord in song. His songs were in English. sometimes repeated afterwards in Welsh in the next meeting, but the appeal did its work, and many souls responded. There was one thing in this meeting which left a lasting impression upon us. The minister of the chapel, evidently an earnest soul-winner, did not seem to understand "the way of the Spirit" as all the ministers we have seed did, standing aside until the Holy Spirit should need. them. This good man seemed to think he must test the meeting himself. Consequently he stopped the proceedings and commenced to urge souls to come to Christ in the way so well known to us. This may have been used much and often, but God is doing a new thing now. The whole meeting fell flat, and without anything to account, for. it the people began to go out in hundreds. Then Mr. Sidney Evans said how God was riot working, and only those who meant definite work were to stay. The minister left the. pulpit, and the power of God returned. A way of working which may be Divine at one time, may not be the way of the Spirit at a time like this.

The fourth and last meeting we attended in Abertillery was in a Welsh chapel, almost wholly in Welsh, but full of holy unction and heavenly fire. The consciousness of God's presence was overwhelming, and there was no need to press souls forward, they shouted out from different parts of the chapel, "I will come to Jesus," and gave name and address out loud, which the minister wrote down. God had the complete control.

Next day we went to Newport, Monmouthshire, and there attended a precious meeting in a Welsh chapel, where the same spirit breathed. We were now in England, and there was a good deal of English in the meeting. We heard in shops, in the streets, etc., of the blessing which God is pouring out in Newport. Lacking something of the Welsh emotionalism, the prayer spirit which was in evidence quite made up for it, and the cry that God will bless England, and especially London, went up from many. In several places in Newport a continuous work of soul-saving is going on.

It was very striking on Sunday to see the quietude of the streets; this is the same wherever the revival has fully taken hold. O God, pour out Thy Spirit upon all flesh, for His sake who so loved the world! Amen.

9: What I Saw And Heard in Wales
By Rev. E. W. Moore, M. A.
(Clergyman of the Church of England, Wimbledon)

"When the Lord turned again the captivity of Zion, then were we like unto them that dream." -- (Ps. cxxvi. 1.) If the Psalmist had penned this verse in South Wales to-day, it could not be more appropriate to the state of things around us. The awakening in these quite valleys and hills must be seen to be realised, and when seen it seems too good to be the sober fact it really is. How shall I attempt in a few lines to describe what I have seen during the last three days?

The very first thing that strikes one is the absolute "liberty of prophesying" which characterizes the meetings. There is no leader, and yet there is an unseen control. "The clock," says Evan Roberts, "no longer determines the time of the meetings." It is quite true they may be announced to begin at a certain hour, but it would be almost true to say they have no beginning and no end. The meeting is in full swing with prayer, praise, and testimony, hours before Mr. Roberts arrives; and if another meeting is to follow in the evening, it frequently continues after he has left. No one is asked to speak, sing, or pray; all are invited to follow the guidance of the Spirit. The missioner himself is constantly interrupted in the course of his address.

Sometimes his words are drowned in a chorus of song, sometimes by the liquid notes of one of the soloists accompanying him. But there is no sense of discord, no break in the harmony. It is like the progress of a stream, now gliding peacefully through the pastures, now thrown into living disorder in the rapids, but whether in storm or calm, still flowing always to the sea.

In Wales everyone nearly knows how to sing. Children of nine and ten frequently can read music. The singing in these meetings is phenomenal. Choir? No doubt there are choirs, but in these gatherings the whole congregation is the choir. If one ventured a criticism at all, perhaps it would be that there is almost too much singing. There was not so much exposition of Scripture as we are accustomed to in England, yet the Scripture was never omitted, and its truths were the burden of every song.

Another most remarkable feature in these meetings is the number of men who attend them. By far the greater proportion of the audience are men, and most of them young men. No doubt the youth of the missioner and the fact that he is one of themselves, is a powerful attraction. But it would need something more than human attraction to draw from the lips of young men the public confessions of sin, the passionate cries for mercy, the open avowals of dedication to Christ, which I have heard and seen during the last few days.

Wonderful transformations have been wrought in these meetings. I have myself witnessed scenes of which I can only say that they reminded me of the accounts of apostolic days. In fact, I cannot, and do not, doubt that this Revival is one of the many fulfillments of the prophecy of Joel (Acts ii. 16, 17); and who can tell what it presages for the world?

But what, asks someone, are the 'practical results of the revival? Praying, and singing, and testifying are well; but does the work end there? Let me give in reply one or two incidents which have come under my personal notice.

Only yesterday a gentleman known to me told me that the doctor of the little village in which our conversation was taking place had surprised him by saying: " Well, the revival is doing me good, anyway. "In what way?" asked my informant. "Do you mean that you have more patients?" "Not at all," was the reply; "but £23 due to me, which I had written off my books as hopelessly bad debts, have been paid to me since the revival began."

Take another instance: The traveler of a certain firm in South Wales had ten years ago a grudge against his employers, because expenses incurred, as he maintained, on their behalf, amounting to £5, had not been paid him. Some months after a mistake was made in a balance-sheet issued by the firm, which put £3 more than he was entitled to receive into his pocket. He saw the mistake at once, but he argued:

"No, they owe me £5 really. I shall let this £3 go against it." This was ten years ago. He was a professing Christian at the time, but ever since then, whenever he attempted any Christian work that £3 came up before him, and he could not do it. A short time back the revival came to his church. He was acting as sidesman, or in some similar capacity, and he asked a passer-by to come in and attend the service. "Not I," said the other. "The people inside are no better than I am." It was a common taunt, but it went to his heart. It was true the man was no worse than himself at any rate. For was not he a thief? He could get no sleep that night, and the next day he opened communication with the firm which he had long since left. The money was repaid, and a breach between himself and his former employers, which had lasted all these years, was finally healed.

Such evidences of the reality of this work could be multiplied indefinitely; all Wales is ringing with them.

There is no question as to it being a work of God. The question is, How is it going to affect ourselves? What blessing, it may be asked, does it bring with it to those who are already Christians? What supreme lesson does it teach? I have no hesitation in giving one answer, at any rate, to such questions. This revival furnishes an illustration of the constraining power of the love of Christ. The young man whose name is on every lip, and who, though on this dizzy pinnacle of notoriety, has not only not lost his balance, but is thus far, at any rate, safe hidden in his Master's shadow, what is his secret? I believe if he were asked he would answer in the words of St. Paul: "The love of Christ constraineth me." He has had a vision of Calvary -- interpret the words as you will. He has seen

One hanging on a tree,
In agonies and blood,

and the sight has enthralled him.

He can see nothing else in comparison with this sight. And the Spirit, the Spirit of Calvary, the Spirit of the Divine Love, has descended upon him, and has made that young man what he is to-day -- a transparency through which Christ shines upon souls around. If we as teachers and workers are to learn an abiding lesson from this revival, it is here: What we need is a fresh vision of the Cross. And may that mighty, all-embracing love of His be no longer a fitful, wavering influence in our lives, but the ruling passion of our souls.

10: Striking Testimony of Eyewitnesses
A CHRISTLY CHRISTMAS

A correspondent writes of what he saw at Christmas-tide:

"It can truly be said that the Christmas of 1904 was the first real Christmas many children -- yea, men and women -- of Wales ever had. Money usually spent in the public-house has purchased groceries and Christmas toys; and where in previous years there has been poverty, with its concomitant misery, this year there was plenty and joyfulness. The Light of the World had entered over twenty thousand homes of fair Cambria and had illumined them with His gracious presence.

"On Christmas Day practically the whole of Wales was on its knees. Probably every chapel in the principality was open, and was filled. In some towns which I visited there were monster demonstrations. Certain churches had combined for united processions, and in some cases the paraders marched the whole night long.

"Inquiries of the police showed that not a single prisoner was detained throughout the holidays. The officer in charge of the Miskin district, a large and populous portion of the Mountain Ash area, said that he had been stationed there for the past ten years, and that this Christmas time was the quietest he had ever experienced.

"In a small colliery in the neighborhood an official said that on several occasions, from the time he entered the workings in the morning until he left in the evening, he did not hear a single oath uttered by any of the work men. At Nazareth English Baptist Chapel, Mountain Ash, 100 young men and women converts of the revival were baptized on Thursday and Sunday. At Aberavon re-markable meetings were held during the festive season. When the pastor of Tabernacle (Congregational) Chapel asked someone to step forward and read a portion of Scripture at one of the services in that chapel a deacon walked to the front and read the parable of the Prodigal Son. 'That parable was fulfilled in my own home yesterday,' he said. 'My own son, of whose whereabouts I have not known anything for the past six months, came home to beg my forgiveness,' And as the venerable deacon told of the welcome home of the son tears trickled down his face."

MR. ROBERTS AND THE INFIDEL

The Rev. D. M. Phillips, of Tylorstown, writing to the British Weekly (London), describes a scene in which Evan Roberts himself figured:

"The evening service at Ebenezer (Congregational) was a never-to-be-forgotten one. Every corner is filled, and the audience is at least 1,000; and three other chapels are packed at the same time. Now, fancy Evan Roberts, a young man twenty-six years of age, facing this audience! He has only an ordinary education, has not a melodious voice, has but very few strains of oratory, and is far from aiming at creating any sensation.

"When an ebullition of emotion is manifested he does not take the least advantage of that, and keeps his mental and emotional equilibrium perfectly balanced in the greatest excitement. This meeting, however, is the greatest test on him in the whole series. But he is a complete master of his position. At the end an infidel was dis covered in the audience, but he did not wish to own that publicly. This was communicated to the revivalist by a young man who spoke to the infidel in the seat. In an instant Roberts was on his feet, and asked the atheist to stand up to express his unbelief in God's existence.

"For some time he refused, but Roberts in a firm manner and in the best feeling insisted that he should. At last he reluctantly got up and said, 'I believe in my heart there is no God.' In a moment a voice from the gallery shouted, 'Out with him,' and there were scores ready to obey the voice; but no sooner had the words dropped from the lips of those in the gallery than the revivalist said in a firm, loving voice, 'No, let us pray for him.' In less than a minute more than thirty were on their knees on behalf of the poor atheist. This was the most dramatic scene that I have ever witnessed in a place of worship. A young man followed the denier of God, and he promised, with tears in his eyes, to take the Bible with him to bed that night to try and get the light. In another ten minutes two other incidents similar to this occurred, with regard to the Deity of Christ and the atonement. These were cogently dealt with in less than five minutes by the young revivalist in such a Christian spirit that I shall never forget it. When these oppositions began to pour in a number of us ministers were trembling, but seeing them disposed of in such a masterly way we praised God, from whom all blessings flow.'"

NO NEED FOR CLOCK OR ORGAN

The Rev. Thomas Davies, of Pontypridd, puts the situation in his church in a few striking words:

"To my church and congregation and the neighborhood the revival has been and still is a great blessing. It is difficult to write about it -- the tears come and one has to stop. The church has been thoroughly revived; we have prayer meetings every evening, and these last from two to three hours. I generally give out a hymn to begin; then the meeting conducts itself. There is nothing to which the most fastidious could object; men and women, old and young, take part, but there is no confusion, and when feeling is overpowering there is deep silence; but the tears are tears of joy, for it is of Calvary we sing and to Calvary we look. There are two things that used to be indispensable to us which we can do without now -- a clock and an organ. The hours slip by without knowing to us. We generally leave the chapel about 10 p. m., but we carry the meeting with us to our respective homes, and on many a hearth there is prayer, Bible reading, and hushed singing going on until the small hours of the morning.

"At Cardiff a young man, who had been lost to his parents for three years, turned up at the very service where his father (a county magistrate) and his mother were praying for him. His father knelt at his side to help him to Jesus, but the son did not recognise him till they both rose to give praise. They then went together to find the mother, who in another part of the chapel was earnestly praying for her lost boy, and who was totally oblivious of anything and anyone around her. The scene was indescribably pathetic, and the joy of all was ecstatic.

"At one of Evan Roberts's meetings a young man told how he spent his early years at Oxford in training for a monk. He ran away to sea, and was absent for twelve years. He settled in Wales, and spent all his leisure in drinking clubs and similar resorts. A month ago, when on his way to his club, he was pressed to go to chapel by a friend. He absolutely refused, but on repeated pressure by his friend he said: 'I'll toss for it. Heads, I go to the chapel; tails, I go to the club.' He tossed, and it came heads. He went to chapel, and he was there and then converted. This was a man well known in his own town.

"In the Coegnant colliery 200 haulers and miners joined in prayer and praise. Those who desired to con fess Christ were asked to signify the fact by holding their lamps aloft. Lamps went up by the score."

STRIKING INCIDENT AT BANGOR COLLEGE

In the course of a smoke-room conversation at Bangor University college last week, among half a dozen of the students, one of them touched on the subject of the revival, expressing the opinion that it was a real thing. A second student thereupon started a hymn tune, another prayed, and ere long hymns and prayers were in full swing. The singing attracted other students, and presently the smoke-room was crowded to its utmost capacity. The students "cut" lectures, and remained in this impromptu prayer meeting from 11 to 1.30. In the afternoon from 300 to 400 of the students attended a prayer meeting at one of the chapel school rooms, at which five lady students in turn engaged in prayer. At night the students formed a procession and marched, singing, through the streets to the Tabernacle, the largest chapel in the town, which was soon filled with a fervent crowd of worshippers. The interest of the students is remarkable, as hitherto they have, as a body, manifested no particular interest in the revival.

NO DRUNKENNESS CASES FOR TRIAL

Striking evidence of the effect of the revival in the villages surrounding Wrexham was given at the Wrex ham County Petty Sessions last week, when the magistrates, who generally sit for two or three hours, concluded their business in an hour. There was not a single case of drunkenness to be tried. The coal-miners working in the Rhosddu colliery sing hymns in descending the pit, and in ascending after their work. They also spend part of the time allowed for meals in prayer.

CONFESSION OF A DESERTER

A Welsh convert induced an English friend to accompany him to a revival meeting at Ammanford. The Englishman ultimately rose and thanked God that his eyes had been opened. The following Sunday he went to the English Wesleyan Chapel, and, to the surprise of all, declared that, seven months before, he had deserted from his Majesty's Navy. He afterwards gave himself up to Police-Inspector Davies, and was taken to Llandilo to await an escort. The churches at Amman ford offered prayer on his behalf. The deserter has since been pardoned and a discharge granted.

LECTURE CHANGED TO A REVIVAL MEETING

The Rev. D. Stanley Jones, of Carnarvon, has had a totally unique experience. Mr. Jones is well known as a preacher and public lecturer, occupying what is regarded as the leading pastorate of his denomination in North Wales. He had a long-standing lecturing engagement at Abergynolwyn, a slate quarry district in Merionethshire. The subject of the lecture was a celebrated Nonconformist worthy, and the proceeds were in aid of the chapel funds, everything, in fact, being in the strictest harmony with the religious views of the community. When, however, the lecturer arrived at the chapel, which was densely crowded with an audience of ticket-holders, he was informed that it was the wish of the audience that he should preach, not lecture.

And this he did, the occasion being probably the first on record where an audience had purchased tickets for a sermon. The sermon itself was brief, but the meeting itself lasted for five hours, being transformed into a typical revival meeting.

AMMAN VALLEY CHANGED

Never have such scenes been witnessed in the Amman Valley as those now daily seen in connection with the revival movement. At Bethel Chapel on Sunday 150 new members have been received into church member ship, and at the Baptist Church, Bethesda, over fifty converts. At Gwauncaegurwen the church at Carmel, which seats about a thousand persons, has been repeatedly packed on the occasion of prayer-meetings, and 120 converts have been made, including many who had never before attended a place of worship. Here the women have been conducting special prayer-meetings, and the young people also have been very active, holding out door meetings. Here also a great change in the daily life of the people is noticeable. The owners of drinking houses at this place say their business has been reduced by one-third.

A railway employee testified at Holyhead that it was most delightful to travel along the road now. Everywhere he met evidence of the revival, and the moral tone was altered. Men buttonholed him at every station in regard to his soul's salvation. At Amlwch, at a single service, as many as seventy-five conversions were recorded.

A party of half a dozen Bangor Baptist and other students visited Llangefni on Thursday last. It was market day. They started a prayer meeting in the centre of the crowded market, and the marketing was instantly abandoned, the people enthusiastically joining in the religious service. Mr. William Jones, M. P., associated himself with the proceedings.

Mr. John Williams, one of the South Wales miners' agents, states that the present revival is one of the most remarkable in the history of reform, both in the industrial and the religious world. He has observed a great change in the manner in which the workmen he represents deal with their industrial affairs. He was deeply struck by the spiritual tone of the last district meeting, the climax being reached when one of the delegates arose and, with arms extended, led the meeting in prayer. A thrill of surprise and ecstasy filled all.

At Stow Hill Wesleyan Church, Newport, the Rev. Sylvester Whitehead, president of the Wesleyan Conference, thanked God for the revival, and prayed that it might spread over the whole land. He read of drunkards and blasphemers praising the name of God, of fraudulent men paying their debts, of men who had been separated by long years of estrangement clasping hands in reconciliation, with tears of joy running down their cheeks.

At the annual Congregational Conference in Wales, the Rev. J. W. Price in his presidential address took for his subject, "The duty of the Churches in view of the great harvest gathered in through the present revival movement." He said the churches of Wales to-day had 40,000 converts. What were they going to do with and for these souls? Were the churches alive to their responsibility in this matter? They would probably never again have such an opportunity.

At one place there was a most dramatic incident. All day in the chapel a man of seventy had hardly ceased his prayers that his father, an old man of nearly one hundred, should be converted. Late in the evening, while he was making the final appeal, and was nearly insensible from exhaustion, an aged man, with hair of snowy whiteness, tottered up the stairs of the gallery and was assisted trembling to the front. The offerer of prayer looked up. "Father!" he exclaimed clasping his hand. Silence as of death fell on the congregation. Slowly the penitent raised his head. "All my life," he cried, " I have lived in sin, but at last the Light has come." A shout like a clap of thunder shook the building, and spontaneously the vast audience broke forth into thankful praise.

Two evangelists from London went to the locality where Mr. Evan Roberts was present. The Spirit of God was manifested in a marked degree. Then, travel ling many miles away, where Mr. Roberts had not been, they found similar deeply spiritual manifestations. Unable to get lodgings at a private house, they reluctantly took up their abode at an hotel, where drinking was going on in a bar at the front of the house. "We had better stay," said one of the visitors; "perhaps God has sent us here." The chapels in the district were densely crowded, and the meetings prolonged to a very late hour. It was past midnight before the party returned to the hotel.

About two o'clock in the morning one of the visitors was aroused from his sleep with a message that the landlord urgently desired to see him. The proprietor of the hotel was in his room in deep agony of mind, and exclamations such as "Oh, I'm a great sinner. Tell me how I can be saved," came from his lips. "If you are in earnest," replied the evangelist, "you will cry to God." The man did so, and while the Gospel was being simply and lovingly spoken, he rose from his knees and declared that, great sinner as he had been ("I've been on the drink," he added, "for weeks,") he knew he had now received the Lord Jesus as his Saviour. The next day he made an open confession of Christ, and two men in his employment, who had also been great drunkards, went down on their knees confessing their sins, and professed to find the Lord.

At a meeting at Ponkey, North Wales, an interesting incident took place. In the school-room a children's prayer meeting was being held while the adults met in the chapel. A little boy prayed to God to save his father, who happened to be at the meeting in the chapel, and later the father was found to be among the converts. Hardly a meeting passes at Rhos without a number of conversions, and the approximate number of converts in Rhos, Penycae, Ponkey, and Johnstown up to last week was over 1,200.

Rev. T. Charles Williams, Menai Bridge, says:

"The meetings are characterized by much spiritual fervor, and many dozens have taken part in public worship for the first time. There are over sixty converts. The prayers of the children in some of the meetings have been remarkable in their effect. The revival broke out in this place without any visible human agency, and the movement is not directly guided by any one. The ministers have thrown themselves heart and soul into it. Prayer meetings are to be held every evening this week, and the Welsh Methodist Chapel, the largest building in the place, has on more than one occasion proved too small. The force and reality of the movement here is not challenged by anyone, and there can be no doubt that its effect will be lasting and beneficial."

The movement is making great progress at Risca and district, and many conversions are reported: Bethany (Baptist), 130; Glyn (Congregational), 150; Primitive Methodist, 15; Wesleyan, 14; Moriah (Baptist), 300. At Cross Keys: Hope (Baptist), 165; Trinity (Congregational), 280; Primitive Methodist, 130; Wesleyan, 40.

Mr. David Davies, Justice of the Peace and chairman of the Maesteg Council, says:

"As regards sobriety, there is a remarkable improvement throughout the district. A brewer's traveller admitted to a friend of mine that his returns had fallen seventy-five percent. The 'tone' of the district has undergone a great change, the street language being much improved. The stillness of the early morning is broken by the hymn-singing of the colliers going to and returning from work, and late at night the air is full of the singing of revivalists going home. There is practically no police work now, as quarrelling and drunkenness seem to be almost at an end. The chapels were never so well attended. I know dozens of men who had previously simply squandered their money, but who are now spending it on food and clothing for their families. Children who before could not attend Sunday -school for the want of decent clothing and cleanly attention are now flocking to the schools, well shod, neatly clothed, and with clean hands and faces. I have lived here all my life, but have never seen the houses and the children so well cared for."

Ystalyfera has been strongly influenced by the movement. Prayer meetings are held nightly at all the chapels, and between two and three hundred converts are reported. The scene on Sunday at a communion service at Wern Chapel was striking. First the women, then the young lads, and then the elderly people marched up the aisles of Wern Chapel to be accepted into church membership. The large congregation burst forth into praise, and many wept with joy. A converted driver, asked why he looked on so patiently at the break down of his cart, said: "If this had taken place a fort night ago I would have cursed enough to set every lump of coal afire, but that is now stopped by another fire burning within me."

Incidents without number might be added, but these, thus hastily gathered together, sufficiently indicate the remarkable character of this most impressive movement. Christian people in America will pray that the divine fire may spread not only throughout other sections of Great Britain, but, crossing the sea, may awaken the churches of our own land, leading forth a mighty host of the Lord's people "willing to bend" (to use one of Evan Roberts' favorite expressions) to their Master's will and be "obedient to the voice of the Spirit."

Made in the USA
Coppell, TX
02 September 2020

35839203R00094